Orphans
of Katrina

The animals need you, thanks for caring

Orphans of Katrina

KAREN O'TOOLE

GIVE A DOG A BONE

Carefree, AZ

First Edition
Paperback

Cover and internal design © 2010 by Give a Dog a Bone Press

Publisher:
Give a Dog a Bone Press
P.O. Box 5665
Carefree, Arizona 85377
GiveaDogaBonePress.com
OrphansofKatrina.com

Book Design: Ghislain Viau
Editor: Pamela Guerrieri
Book Shepherd: Pete Masterson
Cover photo of Little Boy Rudy: Marie Shannon Peck
Photo Enhancement: Charlotte Bass-Lilly & Diane Walsh

Library of Congress Control Number: 2010905158

ISBN: 978-0-61-532916-1 paperback

Printed and bound in the United States of America

10 9 8 7 6 5 4 3 2 1

In memory of my mother, Rita.
Save me a seat.

"If, reader, you are slow now to believe what I shall tell,
that is no cause for wonder,
for I who saw it, hardly can accept it."

DANTE'S *INFERNO*

Contents

PART 2 — AS THE DUST SETTLED

PART 3 — KATRINA PET PROFILES

RESOURCES

Introduction

The Winds of Change

Everybody was asking questions after Katrina, but nobody was asking the most important ones. Magazines, newspapers, documentary filmmakers all wanted input from animal rescuers, input they thought was revealing: "Why did you go? How did you get there? Do you have a favorite rescue story? Favorite reunion story? *Any* favorite story?"

All valid questions, but not the most significant. New Orleans after Katrina could not be interpreted by the photos and images shown to the outside world. You had to live inside the locked-down, destroyed city to know what to ask. Life inside was so desperate and traumatic that even those of us who lived it had difficulty absorbing it. It was its own unique world, with its own rules, its own code of ethics. New Orleans was suddenly a Third World country— a foreign land so impoverished, so war-torn, so devastated, that we felt like we were thousands of miles outside the USA.

The queries came, but not the best ones. No one asked what it was like to live in a celebrated, vibrant American city that had been reduced to rubble overnight. No one asked what it felt like to walk through vast suburbs, thick with homes, yet never find another person, never see a car move, never hear a bird chirp. No one asked

1

what it was like to sleep on the toxic hot pavement of a parking lot with armed military guards all around so that you wouldn't be killed at night. And most importantly, no one asked what it was like to live in a city full of entombed, dying pets unseen in the houses and apartments surrounding you.

It was a citywide guessing game and we were losing. What was it like? What was it like? What was it *really* like? No one asked.

I spent four months volunteering in New Orleans, then several months working on the Internet helping evacuees track down pets. As the chaos died down, I felt I had done all I could for the people and animals of the Gulf, and I was ready to get back to my own life. But if the media had been on the wrong track with its questions, I would soon discover the more disturbing issue. Books and articles written about Katrina animal rescue were glossing over too much of the truth, hiding the enormity of the tragedy and missing the all-important details that helped explain the largest animal rescue in history.

Despite some dramatic photo coverage and a handful of poignant articles, there were mostly stories about happy pet reunions and glossy photo journals showing animals swimming to safety. I realized the true story might never be told—the true story of a human and animal disaster so far-reaching and heartbreaking that the very people who lived it were burying it.

I thought back to the thousands of animals I had encountered, to the enormity of the suffering they'd endured, and I felt compelled, once again, to come to their aid. Even in their death—especially in their death—theirs was a story that needed to be told. A story of tragedy and triumph, of love and loyalty. Could I return to my own life and walk away now? Could I shut my eyes and ears to all of this? Could I slam the door on the Gulf and never look back?

No. I couldn't desert these incredible animals that had no voice to speak for themselves; no way to tell their own story. Alone, they faced one of the greatest disasters to ever occur on American soil, and most paid with their lives. Who would tell their tale? And who would reveal the desperate plight of the hurricane survivors and the animal rescuers? The impossible challenges we conquered … the grave mistakes we made … the valuable lessons we learned.

This book is my humble, heartfelt attempt to remember the people and pets of the Gulf: a scrapbook of stories, observations, and photos collected from deep within the world of Katrina. It is my ode to the brave pets and rescuers of the Gulf. With their lives, and deaths, they brought needed focus to the desperate plight of the animals we share our world with.

I have a deeper respect and more profound love than ever for the people and pets in our lives. Come on this journey with me, and I know you will too.

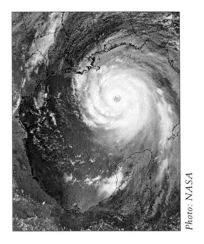

Photo: NASA

August 23, 2005—A tropical storm formed in the Caribbean. By the next morning the storm had the recognizable swirl of a hurricane and was officially named Katrina, the eleventh named storm of the 2005 Atlantic hurricane season. With winds of forty mph she was expected to strengthen to a Category 1 storm as she approached Florida's southern coast.

August 25—Katrina cut across Florida leaving massive damage and nine dead. Intensifying into a Category 5 storm over the warm waters of the Gulf of Mexico, she reached winds of 175 mph.

August 29—Katrina turned slightly eastward before slamming into the Gulf shore, redirecting her most potent winds and rain away from vulnerable, low-lying New Orleans. Now reduced to a Category 3 storm, her western eye wall, the weaker side of her punch, hit New Orleans with 125 mph winds and storm surges from ten to nineteen feet.

August 30—Katrina had come and gone, but the city would suffer a far greater disaster. With breaches in more than twenty levees and floodwalls, 80 percent of New Orleans was underwater. Along with tens of thousands of American citizens, more than two hundred thousand domestic pets were stranded. An estimated 40 percent of the people who stayed did so because of their animals. Many died trying to protect these beloved pets.

Part 1

COME HELL
AND
HIGH WATER

For weeks my home was this handicapped parking spot at the Winn-Dixie supermarket on higher ground in New Orleans. My bed was this oily comforter left behind by a vagrant.

Chapter 1

My Story: From a Suite to the Streets

first met Katrina in a tony white suite at the Mondrian Hotel on Sunset Boulevard in Los Angeles. I may have been the last person in the United States to hear about her. I didn't know she had been a tropical storm in the Caribbean. I didn't know she had rearranged parts of Florida. I didn't know she'd then entered the Gulf and had become a Category 5 hurricane. Katrina had come and gone before I even heard her name.

Though the eye wall of the hurricane slammed New Orleans on August 29, 2005, it was September 2 when I first crossed paths with Katrina. And from that day on our lives would be forever entangled.

I had just checked into my favorite room at the hotel. It was a rainy late night and the city air, thick with humidity and hip-hop, was swirling up from the pool at the Skybar below.

I work as a film production coordinator and you're either on a film set ... or not. I had taken the year off and spent my days boxing and dancing. Odd combination, I know, but every day in the summer I would work out at the old-school Hollywood boxing club, Wildcard, where world champions train. At night I'd study at the Millennium Dance Complex, a Mecca for professional dancers. I was taking Argentinean tango, swing, salsa, and master hip-hop classes from the choreographers of the A-list recording artists. I took flamenco lessons up in Glendale and was bungling through private chess classes. Yep, my curriculum was full. I was taking Hedonism 101. Or maybe 202. Hell, I was going for a full-blown Ph.D. in play now, pay later. But fall was closing in fast and film jobs would be popping up. I already had a trip scheduled in a month to Cambodia to shoot a documentary about orphans in Phnom Penh. Life was good, *too* good—a clue that something was about to go dead wrong.

In my room, I picked up the crisp, white note card folded in the welcome basket of fruit and wine. *Welcome back, Karen. Always nice to have you here.* That's the good thing about being a regular at boutique hotels. You exist. The bad thing: it costs a lot to exist. I was a frequent guest at the hotel that year. It was home to me. Everyone there was my friend, not only the staff, from the valets to the management, but also the recurring hotel guests: that quirky, nomadic crowd of worldwide hotel-hoppers.

If heaven really is decorated in white with billowy clouds everywhere, then the Mondrian copied the look. It's easy to describe the rooms: white-on-white, white goose-down couches, white goose-down bedcovers, white carpet, and white candles with glowing white light. There's a hint of blush on the fresh white orchids and that cashmere throw-thing on the bed that's slightly *off*-white. You can buy one too. For eleven hundred dollars you can take it home and have your own cashmere throw-thing. (A small rectangular throw, too small to keep you warm and too large to wear as a scarf, so ask for a discount.)

I stood on my balcony. The hip-hop from the pool was growing louder. Gazing over the LA skyline in the distance, I thought the same thing I always thought about the city: LA is such a scrawny little city with such a big attitude. The few skyscrapers downtown weren't tall enough to scrape the sky, or even bruise it; they could barely reach it.

I stepped into the living room and flung the curtains shut behind me. Grabbing the remote, I clicked on the TV. A gaunt blonde was speaking: "Sixty percent of all Americans own pets and many own multiple pets." Hmmm. Everyone I knew had pets; either her statistic was wrong, or I only hung out with pet owners. Probably the latter.

Stepping into the bedroom, I turned on the other TV, muting it so I could listen to the animal commentary droning from the other room. But the image on the muted screen stunned me: an aerial shot from a helicopter panning a flooded zone. A flooded city. A flooded *American* city.

I heard the other TV blaring: "Certain regions have more pets than others. It's incalculable how many animals were left behind in New Orleans. No one expected the levees to break."

With two-fisted remotes, I flipped from channel to channel. I walked back and forth between the rooms. Hundreds of channels. One story. Katrina was here.

I was so mad at myself for not knowing. I'd just spent a week at a rental by the beach. I was mindlessly swimming and skating as the Gulf was being eaten alive by a hurricane. Homes destroyed. Lives ruined.

I hated myself. I not only hated *myself*, I hated every person I had met that week. Why hadn't anyone told me? I'd heard the buzzwords *du jour*, like "latte," "Prada," and "personal assistant"— couldn't anyone say "Katrina"? What about the girl at the beach who painted a ladybug on my hand? Couldn't she have casually mentioned the disaster? What about that guy with the dreadlocks who skated past, knocking into me? Couldn't he have said: "Sorry, I was distracted thinking about the hurricane"? And the guy in the convenience store. Couldn't he have handed me my change and said, "Donate this to the victims of the Gulf"? Was that too inconvenient to say? How did I miss this?

It was my own fault for ignoring TV, newspapers, and phones that week. I was escaping from the ever-present buzz, the barrage of useless information. I didn't care what actress was wearing a strapless gown as opposed to spaghetti straps. I couldn't care less who gained ten pounds, and stop already with the endless celebrity award ceremonies. Who cares? They're actors! They're overpaid, over-processed people whose contribution to life is usually nothing more than pretending to be someone else. Am I supposed to celebrate that? Was I crazy to think that maybe we should be celebrating the really important people—the scientists, researchers, inventors? It must be about the wardrobe, I concluded. We could never celebrate scientists. Lab coats and pocket protectors are impossible to turn into fashion trends.

I hated myself. I'd already lost days when I could have been *doing* something. I was meant to be in New Orleans. Coordinating disasters was my real-life job. Movies are nothing more than scheduled disasters with lots of snacks. That's what a production coordinator does—deal with everything thrown at you at once and solve it quickly and efficiently. No matter what comes at you, you've got to handle it. Instantly. You've gotta find endless resources and equipment. Ship countless items. Deal with mountainous paperwork. Move and house hundreds of cast and crew. Get communication systems up and running, offices started. Keep track of what's used, what's needed, what's expected ... what's unexpected. You've got to spin one hundred plates at a time and still catch every new Pyrex bowl whirled at you. The hell with the Federal Emergency Management Agency; Washington needed a film production crew in there.

Yes, I was meant to be in New Orleans. I had spent the entire summer preparing for Katrina. Before I'd heard of her, before she was a nameless gust of wind on a balmy beach in the Caribbean, I was training for her arrival. Between boxing and dancing, I was physically and mentally prepared to enter the fight of my life. I was faster, stronger, and more agile than ever. Was this some kind of destiny thing? Was I *supposed* to be ready for Katrina? Had the heavens demanded I start boxing and insist I buy that silly polyester flamenco shawl?

I flung the cashmere throw-thing across my hotel room. That's how it got the name, I thought. That's all it's good for—to throw when you feel so stupid you can't stand yourself. It was suddenly a bargain at eleven hundred dollars.

Mesmerized, I stood watching the TV: people waving rags on rooftops, helicopters whirling overhead, military convoys trudging through knee-deep water. This wasn't about sending money and hoping someone would take care of it. There wasn't enough money anywhere to solve this. This had to be boots on the ground immediately and lots of them. Including my boots. Definitely my boots.

I watched the helicopter panning the submerged city again. People were being rescued and evacuated everywhere. But their beloved pets *were not*. A cat swam to an immersed tree, clinging to its flimsy branches, then pulled itself out of the tarry water. A soggy dog stood on a truck roof, imprisoned by the deep black water around him. I watched as camera crews floated by on boats. They'll grab that cat, I thought. But no. They'll rescue that dog, I supposed.

But no. They were off to reveal more horror. More pain. And they did, for there was nothing but horror and pain everywhere.

I remembered that commentator on TV. What did she say? "Sixty percent of Americans own pets and many own multiple pets." Her words blended with a helicopter shot of suburban roof-tops peeking out of black water.

If the commentator was correct, that copter just flew over hundreds of pets stuck in those houses.

I couldn't wait to get out of my pure white sanctuary. My goose-down hell. I called the airlines to book a flight to New Orleans. "I'm sorry," said the reservations clerk, "but that airport is closed. I believe it's a morgue now." The extent of the damage was sinking in further.

"I've gotta get to New Orleans. Into the city," I said. "What's the closest airport?"

"Jackson," she replied. "But really, you can't get into New Orleans. The city is shut down. Mandatory evacuation. There's looting going on. Most of the police force has deserted—it's *that* bad. People are killing each other. The roads are closed. It's martial law. The toxic water itself is enough to kill you."

Whoa, I thought. Was this really an airline employee? Or had I accidentally reached the Louisiana governor's office? "Okay, Jackson. I need a flight to Jackson. Where is Jackson, anyway?" I asked.

"Mississippi," the clerk replied. "About 350 miles north of New Orleans."

I worked on the computer all night, reading and writing posts, arranging for boats, volunteers, rides, pet supplies. I flew out the next day to the Phoenix area, my base, to get luggage, clothing, and to buy supplies. As soon as possible I was on a flight to Jackson. Katrina and I were about to meet firsthand.

Plane rides are tough for me. I think too much as it is; lock me in a small, metal projectile and it only adds to the problem. And I had a lot to think about on this trip.

I had fond memories of New Orleans, a city with which I'd had a long relationship. When I was a kid we lived in New York, but for years my parents would take us to Mardi Gras. The good ole Mardi Gras, when floats paraded down Bourbon Street through the heart of the French Quarter and handmade glass beads were tossed carefully, lovingly. They sparkled under the gas streetlights as they came sailing to your balcony. But the biggest fun of all was when you snatched the beads from the air and your eyes flashed through the crowd searching for the person who had thrown them. And sometimes you would find them, catch their eye, and you had an instant to wave a thank you, to remind them they existed, before they were absorbed by the crowd.

We always stayed at the Royal Sonesta with a treasured balcony poised over Bourbon Street. I still have my collection of glass beads from years gone by. I would never have believed that one day I would be on this flight, for this reason. I glanced around the plane. It was nearly empty, melancholy, quiet. I needed a ride into New Orleans and I knew there were no available rental cars in the town of Jackson. I'd already called the airport. Yes, they had rentals cars, but they were all spoken for by FEMA.

I eyed the flight attendant; she was busy explaining to someone that they no longer gave out raisins, only peanuts or pretzels. That reminded me, I would ask for the entire bag of leftover snacks before I exited. You can never have too many snacks in a disaster zone, I speculated.

Grabbing a magazine, I nonchalantly walked down the aisle, pretending to read. I stopped at every occupied seat.

"Excuse me," I whispered to a couple. "You going to New Orleans?"

"No," replied the wife. "Absolutely nowhere near it," her husband chimed in.

I continued on, with the undercover magazine in hand, stopping at another couple. "You heading to …?"

"No, sorry." They shook their heads, already guessing my question.

Stepping away, I leaned against an aisle seat as I gazed down at a young woman flipping through a four-pound *Style* magazine. "You going into New Orleans?" I asked.

"Are you crazy?" she responded with a stunned glare. For the first time ever, I didn't have an answer. I walked back a few rows and plunked myself down in a seat.

Was I crazy? What *was* I doing, anyway? Among other things, I was dragging sixty new flashlights and batteries into a disaster zone to help people and animals when I was probably *too late*. Had I even thought this through? Even if I hitched a ride to the city, could I get in? Would a war-torn soldier just back from Iraq hold an M-16 to my head and shout, "According to rule 45A of the Geneva Convention you are trespassing on illegal territories. Cease and desist!" Would he not care that I had a bag full of pretzels to share? And what does "cease and desist" mean, anyway? Would I be shot for not ceasing and desisting correctly?

I gazed up the aisle to the female passenger who had asked if I was crazy. Maybe she was onto something. I'd *never* thought this through. Wait, I consoled myself. Since *when* do I think things through? I'd never done that before. If I were to sit around and think things through, I'd never go anywhere. I'd stay home and watch TV. I'd swig back a stiff shot of *Oprah* with a chaser of *Dr. Phil*.

This wasn't something you thought through. This was something you did. And since when was I a "thinker-througher?" Me? I'd spent a lifetime playing *Survivor* and winning. Not long after high school I'd moved to the Amazon, trading with the Huaorani Indians when they still enjoyed a well-earned reputation as the deadly, savage Aucas. A well-earned reputation.

I had lived alone on a deserted rock island. A boat dropped me off half a mile out and I swam in, as no vessels would approach the swirling currents and sharp rocks that encircled the island like shark's teeth. I was famous for swimming from St. Thomas to St. John through Current Cut, known for its treacherous waters. I had crewed world-class private yachts on transatlantic journeys, voyaged on a tuna seine through the Panama Canal and around Central America, and worked on barges touring the many rivers and locks of Europe. I'd lived in the Andes, the West Indies, Central America, Mexico, Europe, and traveled around dozens of other countries. Much of my life I lived in Third World regions, among the poorest of the poor. I am an extremist in every way, as happy living on a dirt floor with chickens pecking around as I am burrowed into a pure white goose-down suite. Extremes I can handle; it's the in-between that scares me. The *safe*. Safety is a kind of death, I always thought.

Okay, *I am* crazy, I surmised, as I glanced around the quiet plane, noting all the people going about their lives. Wait a minute! I'm *not* crazy—I'm the sanest person on the plane. I was doing what I believed in, what I thought was right—no matter what the cost. (Only a true extremist can go from thinking they're the craziest person to the sanest in an instant. But then again, I suppose a crazy person can do that too.) What if I saved one person? One pet? To that one person, that one pet, this was the most important journey I would ever take.

I thought about the famous story of the starfish that washed up on the beach. A kid was jogging down the coast one day when he saw an old man plucking starfish off the shore and tossing them into the sea. There were thousands of starfish washed up, dying on the hot sand.

"What are you doing?" the boy asked.

"I'm saving these starfish," said the man.

"But they're everywhere, as far as you can see," the boy argued. "How can throwing a few back matter?"

The old man threw another starfish into the sea. "It mattered to that one," he replied.

I eyed the female passenger again. She was still flipping through that wrist-breaking fashion magazine. She probably cares who's wearing strapless gowns as opposed to spaghetti straps, I thought. She eyed me cautiously as I continued down the aisle.

I approached a lone female. "Are you going to New Orleans? I need a ride."

"I'm exiting off the freeway about a hundred miles north," she said. "I can drop you off there. That's as close as I'm going."

Perfect, just perfect. Except for one small detail …

Clutching my large plastic bag stuffed with pretzel snacks, I watched the empty luggage carousel go round and round. My ride had left me long ago. The few passengers from the plane had departed. And the airport supervisor was searching for my luggage. The suitcases were tracked to Houston, where I'd switched planes. They were expected to arrive the next morning but I wouldn't see them again for three months. Entering a war zone with no clothing, personal items, or supplies was a handicap, but at least now I was traveling light.

That night in Jackson, with the help of the Internet, I tracked down two rescuers driving in from the Carolinas. They picked me up the next morning and gave me a ride into New Orleans. As we drove into the city, we called contacts we had made on the Internet to find out what roads were open and where volunteers were meeting. We landed at the soon-to-be famous parking lot of the Winn-Dixie supermarket—ground zero for independent rescuers.

Using a bag of dry dog food as a pillow, I would live on the streets of New Orleans a total of four months—sleeping for weeks in the dried sludge on the pavement of the Winn-Dixie parking lot. I later moved to the muddy grounds of a destroyed grade school. Once again in my life I was living on the streets and right at home. As the German philosopher Friedrich Nietzsche so eloquently put it: "He who has a *why* to live can bear almost any *how*."

I never did take a feature film job that fall. I never did return to the Mondrian. I never did meet a soldier who demanded that

I cease and desist. But Katrina and I finally *did* meet. I have attempted to tell some of our story in this book. It is the tale of rescuers, survivors, and their beloved pets. Cherished pets, true family members, innocently left behind, alone, to face the one of the biggest natural disasters in American history.

I realize now that every day, for the rest of my life, I will always be reminded of Katrina. Yes, every day, for the rest of my life, she will make sure that I never forget her.

Photo: Sharon K. Powers

Hurricane Katrina caused little damage in New Orleans. But after she left, residents were stunned to see this water suddenly raging through the streets.

Photo: Sharon K. Powers

Within twenty minutes, the same white vehicle parked in Sharon Powers' driveway had floated past and the water inside her house was waist high. These unexpected floods drowned neighborhoods, leaving little time for residents and pets to escape.

Chapter 2

A Day
in the Life and Death
of New Orleans

Take a close look at this picture. What do you see? A flooded
neighborhood? A few ramshackle homes? An air of stillness
and quiet? Photos can deceive. What you are looking at is the
junction where five worlds are about to collide. Five lives about to
meet. Five souls about to crash. And the results will be tragic.

This was my first day in New Orleans. My first hour. Here I
was, up on a ridge, alone, with a dog leash, a gallon of water, and
a bag of dry dog food. I was told there was a boat out there. Two
rescuers were pulling pets off rooftops and releasing them on this

dead grass knoll. There was no room in the boat to keep pets and no time to deal with them, so they were released here, to relative safety on dry land. I was to catch the pets they'd saved.

I listened carefully as I gazed out. Not a sound. Not a boat motor. Not a bark. Not a chirp. Silence. An eerie silence. A suffocating silence. A silence so deep, so thick, you could hear it. You could hear its morbid presence—a loud, gray tone you couldn't miss. And the smell, palpable, an unforgettable stench you were covered in. Soaked in. Your every pore drenched in the nauseating, damp, dark exhale of a dying city.

"Hello! Anybody?" I yelled out.

I thought the boat people would answer or that someone stuck in a house might call out. But I was wrong. A dog replied. A terrified, frightened plea cracked the silence. A frantic howling. This voice wanted to be heard, needed to communicate. And it was clear. It barked a language anyone could have understood: "Help me! I'm alone! I'm all alone!"

"Don't worry," I yelled into the mud-soaked destruction. "I'll find you."

But would I? Where was he? His pleading bark reverberated through the treetops and endless rows of houses. I gazed out, listening. He was calling me from somewhere off to the left, somewhere deep within the neighborhood.

I ran down the canal toward his voice. "You're okay, boy," I assured him. "I'm here!"

Life had whittled itself down to just the two of us. Two beings thrown together by extraordinary circumstance. And right now his life depended on me.

"You're gonna be okay," I yelled. "You'll be all right!"

But would he? This was already six days after Katrina hit. For six days this dog had been alone. No food. No water. Trapped somewhere out there; lost in the noxious, devastated ruin that once was his home.

I hurried toward the sound of his pleas for me to find him. I promised I would. "It's okay, I'm here for you," I called out reassuringly. His barking grew more and more frantic as I came closer. He knew someone was there for him. At last someone had come. I could feel his excitement. Yes, someone had finally come for him!

As I ran towards his voice, I spotted him. There he was, far down the row of houses, his little brown head peeking out an attic window. At last he could see me, too. His whole body wagged.

I waved and shouted, "Hold on. We're gonna get you." He screamed back at me, answering my every call.

And suddenly—he jumped. His tiny body leapt from the attic and splashed into the black water only a few feet below. Holding his little head high, he paddled toward me, leaving a small wake behind him. Struggling through the narrow street of floating debris and hurricane wreckage, he fought his way to me. I cheered him on. He would soon be safe. Soon be held. Soon be cared for. "I'm here, boy. It's okay. You're gonna be okay."

I watched as he approached a partially submerged tree blocking the street. He disappeared from view for a moment behind the immense branches that spread like gnarled arthritic fingers across the road.

And then the wake stopped. His splashing disappeared. His bobbing head vanished. A grim silence and still water replaced him. He was gone.

No! I held my breath, hoping. But the silence persisted. I screamed to him, "Come on, boy. You can do it. Come to me. You're so close. Please!"

But there was no response. No wake. Too weak to swim to me, he never made it. But he tried. I will always remember how hard he tried. How happy he was. What hope he had in those last moments of his life.

I never had time to grieve for him. My eye caught movement to the right. A dog raced up the canal toward me. A skinny, white dog. A pit bull. He was charging at me, his pale pink tongue dripping from his mouth as he scampered.

The boaters may have let him off somewhere down the levee or perhaps he had swum to shore from a rooftop in the submerged neighborhood. It didn't matter. I was his only hope and in some way, after watching the little brown dog die, he was my only hope too.

Spotting a plank of soggy wood on the ground nearby, I dumped the dry dog food out and poured the gallon of water into a dirty ice chest that had floated to shore. "Come on, boy," I urged him. But the dog had no interest in food; he ran straight at me and lunged. Jumping up, his muddy paws on my shoulders, he licked my face. Food wasn't important to this starving dog—human contact was. I barely had time to pet him, console him, when a helicopter came up over the ridge.

The sound startled the dog and he raced off back in the same direction he'd come from. I called and started out to him, but it was too late. I watched as he ran, clumps of mud flicking from his feet as he disappeared down the ridge. I told myself it was "okay," that he was safe on land, and that others would find him. I was naïve. I was wrong. Being my first day, I didn't yet realize that *there were no others*.

That's when I noticed them. The cats. There, on the roof of the small aluminum shed. Two black cats pulled themselves up through a hole in the attic, then sauntered across the roof to the tall, green tree. Climbing down through the foliage, they slid into the black toxic water and swam toward me. Swam like Olympians.

I grabbed the corner of the wooden plank and dragged the dog food closer to the water's edge. The cats emerged from the water and picked at the food. In no time, they gingerly slipped back into the oily sludge and swam off.

They climbed up the tree onto the safety of the roof. I watched in horror as they exhibited typical cat behavior, licking themselves, cleaning off the toxic, chemical-laden floodwater—a poisonous brew that would soon kill them.

At this site I never did find the boat people or any other animals. Within minutes my rescue partner came by to pick me up and we hurried off to another area.

I would never have time to return to this hidden spot again to feed these cats or search for the pit bull. With few rescuers in town during the flood days, and pets dying everywhere, no one ever would.

All that I have left of their lives is this picture. A junction where five worlds collided. Five souls crashed. May they all rest in peace. And may I forgive myself for never returning to help them.

Rescued pets are caged and cared for near the Lower Ninth Ward in New Orleans.

Chapter 3

The Who, What, and Where of Rescue Groups

Volunteers came to the Gulf from all over the country and the world. Yet immediately following Katrina, the region was so dangerous that precious few volunteers arrived. The nonstop media coverage revealed the horrors of the Gulf, and there she was, the center of attention, New Orleans. The Big Easy. An American gem, a historical, cultural city, suffocating under billions of gallons of sludge.

The city was shut tight. There was martial law, gun-toting looters, murders, and military lockdown. Dead bodies were seen floating by and the poisonous water itself was said to surely kill you. All roads into the city were either destroyed, or blocked by armed military. Yes, the city was shut tight.

Yet while residents were fighting to *get out*, a handful of volunteers were fighting to *get in*—no matter the cost. Once again I was reminded of that quotation from Nietzsche: "He who has a *why* in life can bear almost any *how*." And animal lovers definitely had a why. Having seen one too many pets swimming for their lives, locked in homes, or being ripped away from their owners, they definitely had a why.

Within twenty-four hours of Katrina, volunteers began sneaking past checkpoints and traipsing over crumbling bridges to help the people and pets of the Gulf. But while New Orleans was a hard shell to crack for independent rescuers, it was logistically impossible for the big national groups to set up inside the city. To over-simplify, the bigger the group, the more volunteers, employees and equipment, the further up out of the city they'd have to camp.

Fortunately, anticipating Katrina's arrival, New Orleans' own shelter, the Louisiana Society for the Prevention of Cruelty to Animals (LA/SPCA) located in the soon-to-be crushed Ninth Ward, evacuated to Houston with all of its 263 pets. Across the river in Algiers, the Humane Society of Louisiana (HSLA) evacuated to Tylertown, Mississippi with 157 pets. Luckily, the HSLA had just purchased three acres of land in Tylertown, which became Camp Katrina, rescuing and receiving hundreds of displaced pets.

Soon after the disaster, the LA/SPCA returned to Louisiana and joined forces with the Humane Society of the United States (HSUS), and the American Society for the Prevention of Cruelty to Animals (ASPCA), north of New Orleans at the Lamar Dixon Center, in Gonzales. An equestrian and expo center, Lamar Dixon could handle up to 1,300 animals at a time. Yet some days over 400 pets would be brought in. With constant overcrowding, the HSUS was ordered to stop animal intake. Fortunately, another group, Pasado's Safe Haven, had set up camp not far away, in Raceland, Louisiana, and took their overflow.

Immediately following Katrina, Best Friends Animal Society opened a temporary shelter at the St. Francis Animal Sanctuary in Tylertown, Mississippi, and Noah's Wish set up in Slidell, Louisiana, both rescuing and receiving thousands of pets. Part of Louisiana State University (LSU) was also turned into an animal rescue and triage campus, and the HSUS created an additional camp in Hattiesburg, Mississippi.

Though many volunteers lived and worked at the large tented campuses of the big northern groups, individuals were banding together down in the city and starting their own groups.

New Orleans and environs became sprinkled with fledgling rescues; grassroot sites such as Jefferson Feed Store, two Camp Luckys, Winn-Dixie, and MuttShack Animal Rescue. Later, in October, when many of these camps were shutting down, Animal Rescue New Orleans (ARNO) started up.

In most northern camps, as in the small city camps, only a handful of people had previous disaster or aggressive animal training. In the national groups only these individuals were allowed to "go rescue" in the city. The majority of northern volunteers were not permitted to do hands-on rescue. They were assigned the daunting but important task of intake, paperwork, and caring for up to one thousand animals.

Although vastly outnumbered by the northern groups, most of the hands-on rescue was done by the volunteers living on the streets of the city. We were inside 24/7. We had no commute time, we got to know the neighborhoods, and we befriended the military, police and SWAT teams camped out all around us. All of us struggling together. We were one of them. We all shared this unique, surreal land, with an unspoken, yet unbreakable bond.

Most northern rescuers coming into the city daily had a very different experience. The New Orleans Police Department

(NOPD) put down their big, boot-covered foot and demanded that incoming rescuers hand in driver's licenses and be given background checks before entering the city. HSUS volunteer rescuer Annie Lancaster recalls: " I had to carry a letter from the police chief with me at all times. It had my driver's license copied into it, and I had to show it at every checkpoint—sometimes seven or eight of them—just to get into the city."

Sometimes the "up-north" volunteers would desert these national groups and join us in New Orleans, stating they were tired of "the politics and the rules." (Anyone who marched into the Gulf was probably *not* someone who wanted to follow rules.) Inner-city volunteers were often referred to as "renegade" rescuers, a title that both annoyed us and made us proud. Go figure.

While I've focused mostly on the greater New Orleans area, we are grateful to the many lone volunteers and small camps that set up all over the Gulf Coast to help Katrina's animals. The ASPCA estimates that over 200 small groups would make camp on the Gulf.

All rescue centers, whether the large nationals or the inner city, consisted of an ever-changing corps of volunteer vets, vet techs, animal care workers, and rescuers. While the biggies might have one hundred or more volunteers, inner-city camps might have as few as three or four, up to a few dozen.

As time passed and the Gulf stabilized, more and more rescuers ventured into the region. Unfortunately, as in all disasters, when help was needed most—immediately following the tragedy—there were the fewest people and least supplies.

Once animals were rescued, they were brought to your own base camp (wherever you slept at night) for emergency care. If you lived in parking lot at the Winn-Dixie supermarket, you'd bring pets there. If you lived at MuttShack, based in a destroyed grade school five miles away, you brought pets there.

Although there were always politics involved, small camps usually traded precious equipment and resources among themselves. Unfortunately, national attention and funding was focused on the large groups while the inner-city camps struggled. Early on at Winn-Dixie, our only resource to feed animals was the pet food scavenged from the shelves of the supermarket itself.

Once given emergency treatment the pets were caged and cared for, waiting to be shipped to the larger temporary rescue sites up north, or transferred directly to nationwide animal shelters and foster homes.

While most of the big groups stayed on the Gulf until October, Best Friends stayed the longest, closing their Tylertown center up north and moving closer to New Orleans, occupying Celebration Station, in Metairie, a suburb of New Orleans. They remained on the Gulf until mid-February. The street corner group Animal Rescue New Orleans (ARNO) was taken over by locals and is still assisting Gulf pets today.

Photo: Chris Gubbels

Recycling at its finest: Crates are returned to me after being used to ship cats from New Orleans to the Best Friends rescue center up north in Tylertown, Mississippi.

We Can Make a Difference

America is a generous, caring country that came to the aid of the Gulf full force. Like myself, most rescuers, relief workers, and survivors had never been on the receiving end of charity, never needed help themselves. We were overwhelmed by the support of this nation.

I know firsthand that both during disasters, and in the day-to-day overcrowded animal system, it's the small groups, rescuers, fosters, and sanctuaries that need help the most, yet are always underfunded. We must remember these groups. Think locally ... help is needed all around you.

How can you help? Visit local shelters and no-kill groups and pick one you believe in. If you have no extra funds or goods to donate, you can help by volunteering to walk dogs, care for cats, or foster pets in your own home. If you have little room to care for large pets, consider fostering kittens and puppies. Every spring, shelters are overwhelmed with newborns. Unable to adopt them out due to their young age, they are among the first to be killed. If you foster, you provide their only chance. Dogs, cats, puppies, kittens, ferrets, rabbits, gerbils ... take your pick. They're all in need, right there, in your own community. You can make a difference.

Almost three weeks after Katrina, the military checked this home, informing us of this dog.

Chapter 4

The Writing Is on the Walls ... Cars, Windows, Stairways ...

Everyone on the hurricane-stricken Gulf had urgent information to impart to others. Buildings themselves became centers of communication, massive bulletin boards that told dramatic stories.

Trapped residents wrote pleas for help, while business owners warned looters. The military, police, and other search teams spray painted giant Xs to denote the status of the building, whether it had been searched, or not, and any human remains within. Inside the Xs were coded messages. The noon position held the date, three o'clock for notes, six o'clock the number of corpses found, and nine o'clock, the initials of the search team that inspected the building.

Deciphering the search team was often easy with initials such as: SWAT, DEA, NOPD (New Orleans' Police Dept.) but at times the initials were enigmatic, as some military units used code names. For example, a house checked by the Arkansas National Guard was marked GS for *Gunslinger.*

Animal rescuers communicated legions about the status of animals in or around the buildings. Though few military units informed us by marking homes when pets were inside, word spread among evacuees outside the city that all buildings were being marked. While I was hospitalized for cat bites in the Jefferson Memorial Hospital, I overheard a survivor tell a nurse: "I'm not worried. I heard they mark all the houses when pets are inside so animal rescuers can find them." This was not true. Few homes were marked informing us of animals inside. Finding pets was a guessing game. We had no real way of knowing where they were.

Any "E" designation on a building was always a bad sign. N/E (no entry), EO (exterior only), and E or EXT (exterior) all meant the building had not been entered. Sometimes vast developments were "E" neighborhoods, with homes unopened by search and rescue. Officials merely banged and yelled, listening for a response before moving on. Even massive military units, plus police and government workers from all over the nation, didn't have time to open every house. For the handful of animal rescuers in the city, getting inside these locked homes was a daunting task.

But we *had* to get inside. Most homes were now sweltering tombs for countless beloved pets.

As the saying goes: *If only these walls could talk.* On the Gulf, they could.

We Can Make a Difference

There should be a standard symbol used by search and rescue to inform animal rescuers when animals are seen in buildings. Perhaps something as simple as an inverted W, representing animal ears and the number of animals, such as: Wx4 or Wx2. It's fast, simple, and uses little precious spray paint.

Search teams must always leave buildings opened once checked. Cats raced into hiding when patrol units burst into their homes. Too often screen doors were closed after the building was searched, leaving the pets inside with no exit points. It was common (and devastating) to find animals left behind in homes that had been opened, walked through, then closed up again.

Photo FEMA/Patricia Brach

This house was checked on 9/11 with the dreaded "E" designation: an N/E, or no entry. This explains why so many dead weren't found until months later, when homes like these were rechecked. There wasn't time to break into every home, so both humans and pets died inside.

Photo: Nancy Cleveland

This is a sad tale. On 10/4 a "shy shepherd" was hiding under the house so rescuers left food and water (F/W). On 10/7 passing rescuers take over, leaving more F/W even though the dog is "not seen." Finally on 10/15 the dog was found "DOA" dead in the side yard.

Photo: Geralyn Pezanoski

This aptly named Hell House was the heartbreak of rescuers, since they felt this was preventable. Had the owners contacted a newspaper, blogged, or alerted Web groups that there were more than a hundred animals trapped, someone would have gotten there. If you must leave your pets behind, you can make yourself heard. (Seeing the message on the car, the owners replied on the wall: *Trespassers will be shot. Survivors will be shot again!*)

Photo: Nancy Cleveland

Once these owners returned home, they alerted rescuers that their pets were safe with: DO NOT REMOVE DOGS. Most homes were in shambles and rescuers would find pets outside and take them to makeshift shelters, thinking they were alone, even though their owners were back home. I know of one family that was reunited with their dog, took him back to their home, and then had the dog accidentally rescued again. Unfortunately, this time the dog got lost in the system and his family would never see him again.

Photo: Nancy Cleveland

This dog was first spotted and left food and water (F/W) three weeks after Katrina. Almost two weeks later a neighbor came back and left food. A week later, this lucky dog was back with his owner.

Photo: Dana Kay Deutsch

A rescued Katrina dog awaits his fate in the hands of strangers.

"The greatness of a nation
and its moral progress can be judged
by the way its animals are treated...
I hold that, the more helpless a creature,
the more entitled it is to protection by man
from the cruelty of man." —Mahatma Gandhi

Weeks after Katrina, birds flew back into New Orleans yet were unable to find anything edible—except the dog and cat food left at feeding stations.

Photo: Nancy Cleveland

Chapter 5

Doing the Math

Nobody will ever know how many domestic animals died on the Gulf, caught in Katrina's wrath. In New Orleans alone the numbers range from a conservative 50,000 up to a more logical 200,000—yet the number used most by the media is 50,000. I asked Robin Beaulieu, past shelter director of ARNO, why she quotes 50,000 as the number that perished. Her response: "It's way over that, but I don't want to sound sensationalistic. It's bad enough; I don't think people can handle the real numbers."

Let's look at the "real numbers" so we can understand the scope of the tragedy, acknowledge *all of the* animals that lost their lives, and understand the necessity to plan ahead to protect them.

According to the U.S. government census, **454,863** residents lived in New Orleans before Katrina in 2005. Add to that the population of just two bordering counties—65,554 residents in St. Bernard Parish and 28,995 in Plaquemines Parish—and the real numbers of pets left in the region are staggering. And these figures represent confirmed residents only. Adding business travelers and vacationers, it's estimated there were about 1.5 million people in the greater New Orleans area as Katrina approached.

According to the American Veterinary Medical Association (AVMA), 60 percent of American households, or six out of ten homes, own at least one pet and many have multiple pets. Since multiple pets can mean anything from two to over a dozen, the HSUS estimates the average to be almost two dogs per dog owner (1.7) and over two cats per cat owner (2.4), not including reptiles, birds, fish, et al.

With more than 550,000 residents in these three parishes, and with some 300,000 households and 60 percent of these households owning a low average of two pets, there could have been more than 400,000 household pets in the greater New Orleans area. Remember, that 400,000 number applies to domestic dogs and cats only. It does not include the vast number of strays. Nor does it include horses, reptiles, fish, birds, and so on. To avoid being sensationalistic, we will estimate only the cats and dogs; but as you can imagine, any way you look at it, the real numbers, including strays and other animals, are overwhelming.

Assuming that more than half of the residents evacuated and took all of their pets, or remained in the city guarding their pets (a handful of residents weren't forced to leave, or stayed behind in hiding), then at over 200,000 household pets were left "safely" at home during Katrina.

The number of animals rescued is also difficult to calculate. Media estimates range from 8,000 to 25,000. (The HSUS claims that about 10,000 animals were rescued.) While most animals died, some were rescued but became lost in the vast American system of shelters and foster homes. The HSUS estimates that of the pets rescued, only 23 percent were reunited with their owners. The rest are still missing and unaccounted for. It is also unknown how many Gulf pets survived and are now struggling on the streets alone, or were taken out of the region by strangers. Or were finally euthanized because new homes were never found for them.

With at least 200,000 cats and dogs trapped in their homes, and assuming that up to 25,000 pets were rescued, then about *175,000* dogs and cats are still missing, dead, or unaccounted for. Again, this number does not include horses, reptiles, fish, birds, and other pets.

Domestic pets weren't the only animals caught in this disaster. The HSUS estimates that approximately 635 million farm animals were living in Alabama, Florida, Georgia, Louisiana, and Mississippi prior to Hurricane Katrina. Yes, 635 million! Chicken farms dot the region, holding up to a half-million chicks each. Untold numbers of these farm animals lost their lives, some due to Katrina's weather and flooding, but most because they were kept in the cramped buildings of warehouse farms. With the electricity outages across the Gulf, these factory farm animals died from heat, starvation, and collapsed structures. These animals were reported as "economic" losses.

Not only were domestic and farm animals across the Gulf affected, but Katrina also took a toll on zoos, wildlife preserves, aquariums, and oceanariums.

The Aquarium of the Americas in New Orleans lost most of its 10,000 fish and suffered significant loss of life when, days after Katrina, backup generators failed. Nineteen penguins and a few sea otters survived, along with alligators, macaws, raptors, electric eels, sea turtles, and eight large tarpons.

Since the Audubon Zoo was built on the "sliver by the river," some of the highest ground in New Orleans, the zoo suffered no flood damage. However, the big concern for zookeepers was the psychological impact on the animals by the constant buzz of low-flying helicopters.

Photo: NOAA

On August 29, eight Atlantic bottlenose dolphins were swept into the Gulf when a forty-foot wave slammed the Marine Life Oceanarium in Gulfport, Mississippi. Weeks later they were spotted together by National Oceanic and Atmospheric Administration (NOAA) scientists during a routine aerial survey of the hurricane damage. These dolphins, used to human care and contact, would never have survived in the open ocean.

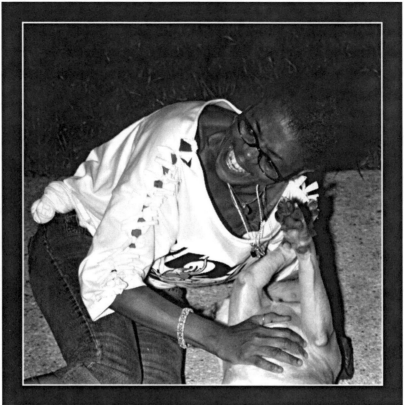

Two Katrina survivors are reunited.

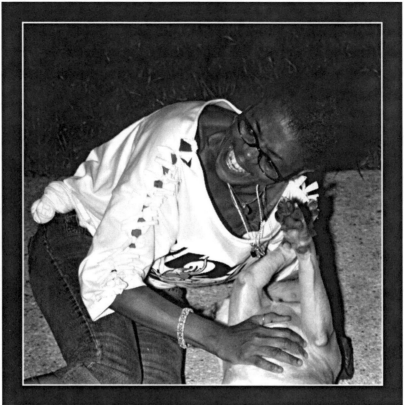 *Photo: Laura Bergerol*

Chapter 6

Animal Rescue Is a People Thing

Any rescuer can tell you that not everyone thought saving Katrina pets was a worthy cause. The more time I spent in the Gulf, the more I heard rescuers discuss others' dismay at their focus on pets, not people. I thought back to when I first flew to the Gulf. A friend called to ask what I was up to. I explained I was on the Gulf , heading to New Orleans to rescue pets.

"Wait, you're going to New Orleans to rescue pets?" she said. "People are dying there. What does that mean—you don't care about the people there?"

"You're not going at all. What does *that* mean?" I replied. Family, friends, and the non pet-loving population questioned some animal rescuers. Somehow, if you helped the animals left behind, that meant that you didn't give a damn about the people. Animal rescue on the Gulf was a classic example of damned if you do, *not* damned if you don't. If you didn't go, if you kicked off your flip-flops, slumped back on your couch, and donated a few bucks to a relief effort, you were okay; you had done your part. But if you dared show up to help animals, some people thought it was wrong of you. For those cold souls, the fate of over two hundred thousand pets, immobilized, dying in a city, was not a serious issue.

For residents, there were SWAT teams, military squadrons, helicopters, boats, aircraft, buses … an army of people and equipment mobilized to find and assist them. For their beloved pets, their smallest family members, the scores of animals they were forced to leave behind, there was no one. These confused, desperate pets, like their owners, had their lives ripped out from under them.

A month after Katrina, I came across a frail, tired man folded over, leaning on his porch rail as he stared at his destroyed home in a ghetto of New Orleans. Spray-painted boldly across the splintered wood of his front door were the simple words: *1 DOG RESCUED*. The man gasped for air as he flicked the occasional tear off his cheek. "They got her," he said. "Rescued her. I was afraid to come back. Afraid of this moment. What if I found her dead? That's all I could think about. For a month now, I hated myself every minute for leaving her."

The man paused, inhaling a wheezy breath. "She was my best friend for eleven years. Maybe my only real friend. I was stuck in

Houston. They didn't let me take her. I imagined her here, inside, suffering. I never slept. She had no food, no water. All alone, waiting. Waiting for me. But I could not help her. I could not get here. Do you understand?"

"I do."

"Look," he read. "Dog rescued. That was my little girl. Someone came and got her. Maybe she thinks I sent someone. Maybe she understands I had to leave her. I hope she knows."

I do not know one rescuer who would trade a day of saving animals on the Gulf for one day anywhere else on earth. I do not know one animal that was saved that wasn't thankful from the depths of its soul. I do not know one Katrina survivor who was reunited with their pet who won't thank God for the rest of their life.

Photo: Dana Kay Deutsch

Chapter 7

Above and Beyond

There were tears in his eyes. I didn't want to see them. He didn't *want* me to see them. But there were tears in his eyes.

Feeling awkward, I glanced away, focusing on the skeletal dog lying limp in the man's folded arms. "We found him on the sidewalk down the road," the man said. "We got here as fast as we could. Will he make it?"

"He'll make it," I lied as I gathered up the dog to rush him to a makeshift emergency room. "He'll be okay."

"I got dogs myself," the man said.

I flashed a fragile smile but still couldn't look him in the eye. I knew if I saw his face, if I saw a tear, I would break down myself. "You may have saved his life," I said.

But I think he knew I was lying. I think he knew it was too late. "We tried," he said. "We did the best we could."

The man paused, gently touching the dog's sticky fur, and then stepped away to the awaiting military Hummer. He was a United States National Guard lieutenant. Dressed in full military camouflage, he was tall, he was tough, he was war-ready ... and he was heartbroken over that little dog struggling to survive. That needy soul that had entered briefly into his life and would exit just as quickly.

Thank God for all the men and women in uniform who were there for us. And *they were there for us.* Sergeants, colonels, lieutenants, captains, privates. Alpha, Bravo, Charlie Company. The National Guard, Marines, Army, Navy, Air Force. Coast Guard, SWAT teams, DEA, police, firemen. Regardless of the uniform, every single one of them, animal lover or not, were all of a collective mind: God help these poor animals.

They waved our pet-laden cars through checkpoints, brought us intel on animals left behind, and helped us move pet food and equipment throughout the city. The military was there to enforce curfew, yet against orders, they would escort us secretly through the dangerous nights, long after curfew had begun. Because they knew. They knew the animals didn't stop dying at night. They knew lost time was the enemy. They knew it was the right thing to do.

Most rescuers had never worked as a team with the military before. As Americans, we had all grown up with images of our military fighting wars in faraway places. We'd seen military bases with thousands of soldiers. We remembered news of camouflage convoys and helicopter squadrons moving through foreign, destroyed regions. But suddenly New Orleans was the faraway place with a war going on. It was the military base with thousands of soldiers. It was that destroyed region pulsing with military convoys.

But New Orleans was a city with no citizens. Except us, the volunteers who fought their way in to help the animal and human survivors. Once inside the barricaded city, we worked hand-in-hand with the military. They called us citizen soldiers.

On behalf of all of us, of all the citizen soldiers who had the honor to work with the men and women in uniform, we thank you. And to that National Guardsman who stopped to assist that dog dying on the sidewalk—that caring man who wanted so much to rescue that helpless being he found struggling to survive—thank you. Because of you, that dog lived. Because of you, he made it.

A white German Shepherd peeks out of an attic window after Katrina.

Chapter 8

How Much Is that Doggie in the Window?

For six thousand dollars you could:

1) Go on an all-inclusive African photo safari.

2) Take a first-class cruise around the Caribbean.

3) Travel to the hurricane-ravaged Gulf, to live on the pavement in the parking lot of a looted supermarket, in an area scientists describe as "having all the devastation of

an atomic bomb, without the radiation." You will dine on sun-melted granola bars and wear the same wet, filthy clothing every day. You will risk your life by being shot at by looters, develop lifelong respiratory problems, and be attacked by lost, scared animals. Here, you will see nothing but death and destruction all day.

For the volunteer rescuers who showed up in the Gulf after Katrina, number three was the only choice.

It cost volunteers a fortune to help save animals on the Gulf. We gave up jobs, flew or drove in, and bore living expenses, travel expenses, and often, too often, medical expenses. While national rescue groups sponsored a handful of people, most of us spent our own money to travel in and live on the streets, working around the clock under horrendous conditions.

Not only did we spend money for our own travel in and out of the Gulf, we also spent vast amounts feeding and treating the animals we rescued. No one showed up empty-handed. Every rescuer came in with as many provisions as he or she could transport—from buying tents, camping gear, and boots, to getting immunizations and buying animal food, cages, crates, traps, leashes, and pet and human medicines.

The list of expenses incurred by volunteers was extensive. Most volunteers spent hundreds or thousands of dollars on supplies and goods for the people and pets of the Gulf. Many rescuers were in over their heads before they even arrived at Katrina-stricken areas, all knowing they would never get a penny back. Most rescuers had no choice but to live on the streets, in tents, or in their cars—or expenses for volunteers would have quadrupled.

Volunteers continued spending large sums of money on extended medical care for the animals they encountered; paying for transportation to fly pets to their relocated owners; and expending countless time and money trying to find animals lost in the system, hoping to reunite them with their families. It was not uncommon, for those who could manage it, to spend tens of thousands of dollars to help Gulf pets. Amanda St. John of MuttShack and Susan Marino of Angel's Gate Animal Hospice each spent more than $75,000 of their savings on supplies and animal health care, with no way to recoup their expenses. The amount of money it cost volunteers in lost wages is incalculable.

Yet we are all thankful that we went. I would not give up one minute of being on the Gulf for time spent anywhere else in the world. Not one minute. For me, not including wages lost, medical expenses incurred, and time spent, it was a six thousand dollar investment in the Gulf. And worth every sweat-drenched, sun-blistered minute.

It was images such as these, of pets being left behind, that motivated animal lovers from around the globe to march into the Gulf.

Breaking this window and entering, we were too late to save the two cats inside. Splits in blinds were clues to dogs trapped inside. They would paw openings to see out.

Chapter 9

The A to Z of
B and E

I studied my objective for a moment. I didn't know much about golf, but I figured for this shot a driver would work best. It sounded correct. I turned to the new rescuer who came out with me that day and said, "I need a driving iron here."

"Huh?" she replied.

"There's a set of golf clubs in the car. A driving iron; I think that's the big fat one."

"It is," she said, caught off guard. "You need a driver?"

"Yeah."

The girl rushed to our rental car and returned with a bulbous golf club. I grabbed it and moved up the walkway to the large front window. With a swing worthy of the Masters, I smashed the plate glass. The center of the window shattered instantly, but the jagged points of glass stuck in the top of the frame and hesitated, as if stunned, before dropping.

The girl was astonished. "You just smashed someone's window with a golf club!"

"Yeah, I would have used a crowbar, but I lost it this morning. It was one of my favorites. They're easy to lose. You break the window and toss the crowbar to crawl in. By the time you leave you forget the crowbar. With all the garbage everywhere they're hard to find later. I found these golf clubs rusting on the floor of a wet garage. They'll have to do for now."

"But you just caused property damage," she said. "I mean, don't you think these people have enough problems without *you* destroying their property?"

"Hmmm. You have a point," I said as I sized her up, not sure if she was just new to rescuing—or also new to the planet. "You're right. Once you remove the tree that's embedded in the roof, tow away the car that's upside down on the lawn, haul off a few tons of garbage from inside the house, and pull down all the interior walls contaminated by mold—that broken window could be a real eyesore."

Breaking and entering wasn't taken lightly. Some rescuers were strongly opposed to it and regarded it as property damage. Rescue outposts that were housed outside the city and sent rescuers in during the day often warned against it. But most rescuers knew that it was essential to saving lives. Pets were locked inside, waiting.

For these pets, our choice—whether to enter or not—meant that pet would either live or die. I had no respect for any rescuer who would leave an animal to die over a broken window. On the Gulf, there were too many dogs lying inside their front doors trying to scrape and chew their way out; too many cats locked in back bedrooms, long without food. Breaking and entering was a skill, a life-saving necessity that had to be mastered quickly.

Some rescuers believed if you broke a window, looters could get in. Did they really think that looters have no problem pillaging homes but that breaking a window conflicted with their high code of ethics? All of our time was spent in low-income developments. Looters weren't hanging around waiting for us to open houses for them.

Many developments were completely locked up. No one had been in them. No entry points. No doors or windows broken or opened. No military markings. These buildings were scorching deathtraps for any pets locked inside.

Windows were usually the best way to get in. Trying to wedge a door open with a crowbar was often futile; the wood around the door frame was so swollen from floodwater that the frame collapsed or splintered from the effort. Kicking in doors was a no-no. "Never use your body as a tool when breaking in," SWAT team members would warn. "You'll hurt yourself, ruin your knees, be outta commission." Only on the Gulf could you get advice on breaking into homes from the police and military.

Forget doors; it was easier to smash a window. There was plate glass, shatterproof glass, and sometimes that deadly Plexiglas, impossible to smash. It would almost break your wrist when you slammed a crowbar into it and the crowbar bounced off.

We usually smashed windows with the screen in to prevent the glass from spraying. Then you could slam the hook of your crowbar into the middle of the screen and yank. The thin aluminum frames bent easily and collapsed as you jerked out the entire screen, frame and all. By reaching through the broken glass and tearing the curtains down off their rods, you could pull them out of the window, creating a fabric layer beneath you to help protect you from glass shards as you crawled in. You'd always break a window closest to a door, in case you could reach in and unlock the handle.

We wore sunglasses and looked away on impact to protect our eyes, but we had nothing to protect our lungs. We all tried to avoid inhaling that thick puff of green smoke, powdered mold, which always burst from the window, as if it had been waiting inside to escape. Later, Centers for Disease Control (CDC) authorities could be seen entering these same buildings in full white space suits with booties, gloves, and oxygen masks. Not an inch of skin exposed. We were usually lacked our flimsy blue face masks; even when we had masks we often did without due to the extreme, suffocating heat. CDC officials warned us we would pay for this someday when we contracted severe mold-related respiratory diseases.

Some of us were really good at breaking and entering. (I was a little *too* good. I must have been stealing Rembrandts in a past life.) You had to get in, get out, and get to the next house. With not a minute to waste.

After breaking the window with my driving iron, I entered the house alone and gazed around. No paw prints in the mud-covered living room to indicate that a pet was loose inside. Passing the kitchen, no visible pet bowls, leashes. But down the hall I could see the closed bedroom doors. Often homes gave us no clue that animals were inside, yet you would find multiple pets locked in bedrooms or bathrooms.

My new ex-friend was standing outside with her mouth open as I reappeared from inside the building. Unfortunately, I came out empty-handed. I remember thinking, "Too bad I didn't crawl out with a cute Yorkie, just to prove my point." But she had seen enough. I could tell she thought I was nothing more than an empty-handed property damager with little knowledge of golf.

But I wasn't finished. We had the whole neighborhood to crack open. I handed her the golf club. "Go break that window, there, across the street."

"No!" She shook her head, appalled that I expected her to aid and abet a criminal.

But there could have been something in that house. There was a white cat figurine in the window upstairs, a clue that the homeowners could be animal lovers. We always looked for clues; we desperately needed help finding the animals, so we developed what the military called situational awareness. We noticed *everything*. Sometimes seeing a cement birdbath on the lawn, or a potted plant with wire butterflies attached, things seemingly insignificant, revealed the personality of the owners and saved their pet's life. Finding a doghouse outside a residence wasn't always a clue. Often they floated from neighboring houses until they washed up with other debris. "Beware of Dog" signs were also misleading, since many people without pets posted these to ward off criminals, which I guess, in this case, was me.

Miss Etiquette refused to break the glass and wanted to leave. Ignoring her, I crossed the street and smashed the front window. Bingo. On the living room table was a bird cage, and in it were two beautiful but skinny lovebirds, huddled together. I searched the rest of the house before grabbing the cage and exiting.

The girl was not impressed. *Au contraire.* I'm sure she was disgusted at the great speed and accuracy with which I could cause property damage. She never said a word but her eyes burned holes in my corneas.

"Did you ever see the movie *Lord of the Flies?*" I asked. She shook her head no. "These proper, educated English boys get stranded on an island, and life as they knew it was over. Alone, with no rules, no authority figures, the surreal becomes the real. They are so far removed from ordinary life—none of them cared about important things, like the difference between a soup spoon and a dessert spoon."

I could tell I was losing her. I was getting lost myself. But it sounded good. "The point is, desperate times call for desperate measures."

I *had* lost her. "Can we go back to base camp?" she said.

Miss Etiquette would soon become MIA. Another rescuer who came to the Gulf with the best intentions but couldn't handle "city" life. Not this city, not under these circumstances. New Orleans after Katrina wasn't right for everyone. But then, everyone wasn't right for New Orleans.

We all met rescuers who drove across country, then stayed a day or two or sometimes only hours, before racing out of town. The long, tough road wasn't *getting* to New Orleans; it *was* New Orleans. You lived and breathed death. At night you didn't go home to relax and recover from a long, heartbreaking day. Home was a cement parking lot where you lay awake, in the open, listening to imprisoned dogs bark to you, call you, dying in random distant houses. Home was where armed military guards with night-vision goggles patrolled the parking lot around you, protecting you from being shot as you slept. Home was *not* "where the heart is." Your heart was scattered in dust-sized particles across the demolished city. There was no relief from the streets, ever.

New Orleans wasn't for the squeamish, the faint-of-heart, or the fearful. It wasn't right for that girl—but she wasn't right for it either.

Then a thought came to me; maybe she *had* seen or read *Lord of the Flies*. Maybe the mere mention of it scared her away. After all, at the end of the story they start killing each other.

We Can Make a Difference

Many pet owners used mass posts on the Internet, begging rescuers en route to the Gulf to enter their homes and save their pets. Some rescuers would arrive with pages of citywide addresses where pets were confined. Unfortunately, not all rescuers had these lists; most had nothing to go on. And with so many emergencies on the way to these list addresses, volunteers were often pulled in another direction, and it could take days to reach those homes.

While laws have changed, making it easier to evacuate your pets in a disaster, if your animals get stuck behind in an emergency, use every resource—the Internet, radio stations, newspapers, phone calls to authorities, anything—to draw attention to your pets. If you don't know how to effectively use the Internet, enlist the help of others. Ask for assistance at your local library or the computer department of any college. Hopefully a situation like Katrina will never happen again, but in any disaster you can make yourself heard.

Photo: Mark Steinway

Chapter 10

Our Hearts Were Broken
a Hundred Times a Day

People warned me, "You don't want to show any of *those* photos. The images are too horrific. The sights you got used to seeing as rescuers, the general public can't handle."

I knew exactly what they were referring to. All rescuers have *those* photos: the haunting images that documented the death all around us. Images so graphic, so powerful, so revealing of the animal's final struggle, that we cannot show them. *Those* photos are the ones we ourselves can barely look at. Pictures that take us back instantly to that time … that place … that pain. It's a hurt so deep, so lonely, so heartbreaking and abrupt, it takes our breath away. *Those* photos are the images that have burned a permanent hole in the heart of every rescuer, one that will never heal.

I think back again to what people said: "The sights you got used to seeing as rescuers, the general public can't handle." We *were* the general public. On August 30, 2005, hours after Katrina left the Gulf, volunteer rescuers, lone soldiers, began their march into the region. We were substitute schoolteachers, college students, secretaries, stay-at-home moms, truck drivers, librarians. We were America. All of America and everything it stood for. We *were* the general public and we were marching in to help our neighbors: the people and pets of the Gulf.

And so we arrived, an army without training. Unlike the military, we weren't schooled to mentally and emotionally handle a war zone; we weren't prepared for what we would see. And the cost to us would be staggering. Some rescuers have since lost their jobs, families, homes, well-being. Some have been hospitalized for nervous breakdowns; most have sought counseling for post-traumatic stress disorder … two that I know of committed suicide.

It is often asked, "Who will rescue the rescuers?" Nobody seems to know. But one thing is sure—we all try to bury the images, the pain, the suffering, the misery, and the hurt of everything we saw … everything we experienced … everything we captured in *those* photos.

These three little angels were rescued together and months later were lucky enough to be reunited with their family.

Chapter 11

My Littlest Angel

She was one of the few animals I rescued that I remember. And even though our eyes met for just a moment, she is one that I will never forget.

Most of us who spent months saving pets on the Gulf remember very little. Day flowed into day, rescue into rescue. While volunteers who were there for short periods of time remember specifics of every animal they saved, for the rest of us, it is a long, shadowy blur. The hourly barrage of pets and the daily onslaught of emergencies are gathered up into one long, painful memory, slightly out of focus. And perhaps it is our own defense mechanism that keeps it out of focus, for the pain of remembering vividly would cripple us.

But I remember her. Vividly.

We were at a low-income apartment complex on Chef Menteur Highway in northeast New Orleans. A two-story, battered brick building with sixty units; a U-shaped structure with a debris-filled center courtyard.

It was four weeks after Katrina and the apartment complex was still locked tight. Any pets left inside were either dead or on the brink. I was with rescuer Gail Posey and a new male volunteer who had just shown up that morning to help at the Winn-Dixie rescue lot.

We raced to check the apartments. Miraculously, a few pets were still alive: two parakeets, a hamster, some fish, all in bad shape but holding on.

Locked in the backroom of an upstairs apartment, I found a frail, scared chihuahua backed against the wall in fear. While I carried the dog out, the male rescuer searched the rest of the apartment.

Animals in tow, chihuahua on my lap, we headed off to base camp.

"Are you sure there was nothing else in that apartment?" I asked the new volunteer.

"I didn't see anything," he said.

"Are you positive?" I wasn't sure why I was asking; it was a one-bedroom, partially furnished unit, not hard to check.

"Yeah," he replied. "There was nothing."

Images flooded my mind, random thoughts. I saw the crusty shower curtain shut, closing off the tub. An empty pet bowl on the kitchen floor. A yellow leash on the table. A stainless steel pet bowl in the hall. Disconnected images. The shower curtain. The shower curtain. The shower curtain.

"There's another dog in that apartment," I said. "I'm positive."

As soon as we retuned to the complex, I dashed out of the car and charged up the steps to the unit. Bursting into the bathroom,

I threw open the shower curtain. And there she was. A whisper of a chihuahua, only two pounds left of her. Her eyes were closed; she lay motionless on her side in the bottom of the cracked, rusty tub. She was covered in swarming roaches that had survived on her feces. I thought it was too late; I thought she was dead.

I reached down to touch her face. Her eye blinked open. She focused on me a moment, then faded back out. And in that blink of an eye, we bonded forever. She will always be my littlest angel, for I believe she called to me, her soul to mine. We were her only chance for survival and we had left without her. We were her only chance to live and we had marched out the door.

We rushed her back to the vet at Winn-Dixie then hurried off to new emergencies, new crises.

I remember watching her as I left her behind. She was laid out on a towel at the vet station, an IV bottle dangling above her. She was unable to move her body, unable to pick up her head. But she followed me with her tiny eyes. We stared at each other as I walked off. And she let me know that I was her angel and I let her know that she was my angel too. My littlest angel.

I do not know what became of my littlest angel. I returned to the rescue parking lot late that night and didn't ask. You learned early on not to ask. In my mind, she survived and right now is somewhere in America, asleep on her owner's lap.

Photo: Liz Roll/FEMA

Days after Katrina, this lucky dog was being cared for by neighbors who had refused to evacuate with their own animals. Unlike this dog that was on a porch for all to see, most pets were locked in, unseen by rescuers.

Chapter 12

Home Alone

I t was four weeks after Katrina and nobody had hit these houses. The entire development was untouched. Not a door open, not a window broken, not a telltale sign of spray paint anywhere informing us that the military had been there.

I was with rescue partner Gail Posey who had picked me up in Jackson, Mississippi, weeks earlier and given me a ride into New Orleans. Gail was from deep within the Carolinas, and her sharp wit and intelligence was seeped in a chowder-thick Southern drawl.

We drove through the development, hidden off the empty highway. The houses were uniform in color as though a mud-drenched brush had painted them all. The debris-covered roads rambled off in every direction on which hundreds of these storm-ravaged houses sat quietly, waiting. Waiting to see what new onslaught of disaster would arise.

This was a dangerous suburb. A low-rent district where most houses had bars on the windows and *Beware of Dog* signs on the gates. These weren't fake warning signs. These homes *had* guard dogs, *needed* guard dogs. And many of these dogs would still be inside. You could smell the finality of death in the air. A boil of dead animals, humans, and rotting food all blended together in this desolate suburb.

Breaking and entering in this development was an enormous task for just the two of us. But there was no one else. Few rescuers were working the streets of northeast New Orleans then. Considering the amount of help needed, few rescuers were working anywhere.

As Gail parked her SUV, I noticed a house down the road—a plain, muddy brick house with tan metal hurricane shutters pulled tight over every window like giant, closed eyelids. The screen doorframe was made of thick steel with heavy, crisscrossed bars welded on—no flimsy aluminum here. Backed up by a solid metal front door, the house was heavily armored. If ever there was a house you *wouldn't* leave a pet in, this was it. It was a metal tomb. A house of sensory deprivation, where neither light nor sound could enter. If ever there was a house you *wouldn't* break into, this was it. With time raging past, and tens of thousands of houses to search, all rescuers had to pick their battles wisely; and this steel fortress was not a wise choice.

Gail and I grabbed our leather gloves and crowbars and stepped into the menacing sun in search of animals. Gail limped across the pavement in her socks. She'd finally removed her boots; her feet were blistered and infected from wearing the same ill-fitting wet boots for weeks.

As we crossed the street, I glanced back at the locked, armored house down the road. I was drawn to it. Couldn't take my eyes off it. It looked cold, stern, impenetrable. But what if …? What if there was an animal still inside? I rushed to the vehicle and scavenged through the piles of equipment on the floor, digging through crowbars, sledgehammers, metal saws, and bolt cutters. Pulling out an ax I sprinted to the house, convinced my intuition was correct … convinced I had little time to save the pet within.

I studied the high windows, lids closed tight with hurricane shutters and locks. I noted the steel front door and barred metal screen as I raced to the back of the house to search for entry points. No easy access anywhere. The house was a stronghold.

Returning to the front door, I hacked into the wooden frame where it met the deadbolt of the metal screen. I slammed down on the wood, trying to cut out the lock, sparking tiny fireworks when I struck metal. Finally I broke open the heavy screen and chopped at the hinge of the metal front door.

I kept pounding with the ax but wasn't getting far. Stopping to listen, I pressed my ear to the door, but not a sound within. Was I wrong? Was I wasting precious time? I was sure there were starving animals locked in the houses all around me, and they were listening, focused on the noise, waiting for someone to find them.

I gazed up and down the long, quiet streets. I remember resting against the building, my arm muscles quivering from the constant swinging of the ax. Tapping on the door, I listened. Nothing. No bark. No meow. No response.

I lifted the ax and slammed it into the door. No matter what, I was going in. After another fifteen minutes, the metal door buckled at the lock, just enough space for me to peek inside. Just enough space to let a stream of sun slip in. Peering into the black room, my eyes adjusted from the bold light outside to the quiet depth of shadow within. And there, staring back at me, stood a dog. I remember when our eyes met. He squinted with pain as the intense light struck him. He ran to me. Sticking his nose out into the small space between the buckled, metal door and the wooden frame, he was whining, barking, licking. A joyful hello, an adoring thank you, a squeal of relief.

Gail saw how happy he was. "He wagged his tail so much," she said, "like he was saying thanks as fast and as often as he could." I still recall his tail pounding on my right leg as he stood beside me, wagging nonstop.

Back at the rescue center, we discovered that the dog was a female, a long-haired, purebred German shepherd—a dog of such high lineage and so well-bred that even weeks of starving in a black, silent tomb could not alter her steadfast, good temperament. The dog was so expertly trained and of such pure lines she would soon land on the cover of a German shepherd magazine, the poster child for the perfect dog.

Unfortunately, even though she had a microchip, the data was not current and her paperwork was sent off with another pet. With no contact information, her owners were never found. Today she is a service dog and lives with a loving family in Southern California. There, she enjoys running in the bright sunlight and listening to the many sounds of nature. For this sweet dog, weeks of being entombed in silence and darkness are all but forgotten. But one thing she has never forgotten is to wag her tail nonstop.

UPDATE: Gail and I would spend days in that neighborhood pulling a multitude of dying pets out of locked houses. Pets that had surely listened, focused on the noise, hopeful that I would find them, as I hacked into that metal door.

We Can Make a Difference

All pets should have collars and microchips to help identify them when lost. Disaster evacuees must update their pets' microchip data when they move, and if their phones are disconnected. Scores of Gulf pets had microchips with outdated contact information, leaving us no way to find their owners. These pets were lost from their owners forever.

A dog clings to the front door of his abandoned home six weeks after Katrina. As we approached, he jumped up and hit the brass door handle, desperate to get inside. We fed him in place for days while in that area, then took him away for safety, as a pack of dogs was then roaming the neighborhood.

Chapter 13

"Loyalty means nothing unless it has at its heart the absolute principle of self-sacrifice."

—*Woodrow Wilson*

H e would have waited there until he died. The front door to his ruined home was wide open, but the dog was still inside. Waiting.

It was four weeks after Katrina and once again something told me there was a dog inside the plain, brick house. We were driving through the ramshackle neighborhood when I heard him. Although he didn't make a sound, I heard him call to me, whisper to me from afar. I don't know why I heard him—I just did.

That happened to me a lot during the early days after the flood. I'm not psychic, I don't have an especially developed sixth sense, but something happened in New Orleans. It wasn't uncommon for rescuers to be "summoned" by animals. The city was quiet, empty; the conditions dire, catastrophic. Pets all around us were locked up, unseen, struggling, their panic evaporating in the stagnant air as we searched for signs of life. Life so difficult to find there.

But I heard him. A silent signal, clear, urgent. He was crying out to me.

And there he was. In the bathroom, sprawled out on the floor. The once hefty Rottweiler, now a sickly, thin creature too weak to stand, too tired to move. He sank into the linoleum floor; a frail, pathetic figure collapsed between the bathtub and the toilet.

Facing away, toward the window, he lifted his head and glanced back over his shoulder at me, then dropped flat on the floor. That was all the strength he could gather as he lay there, waiting for his owners. No matter how long, no matter what the cost, he would wait right there.

We rushed a bowl of water to him but he was too weak to drink. He glanced up at me, a hollow thank you, then closed his eyes, resigned to die right there. But we wouldn't let him die. We raced him to the nearest rescue center. To this day, I don't know what became of him.

Animals all over the city were home waiting, hoping their people would step back into their lives as quickly as they disappeared. We found a Siamese cat on her porch seven weeks after Katrina; her ID tag confirmed it was her address.

A Doberman lingered outside his owner's door, locked out on the second floor balcony of an apartment complex. He was so thin that he now had the cinched, high waist of a greyhound. The muddy stairs told his story, for there wasn't a paw print on them. In weeks, he had never ventured away from his apartment door, where he sat patiently, anticipating his owners' return.

Again and again the love and loyalty of animals would prove itself. Many that were not drowned or carried away by raging floods were home waiting, pining to see their owners again.

You could not leave the Gulf without a newfound respect for animals. To see their bravery in their most desperate days was a lesson to all of us.

As the city swelled with more military, volunteers, utility workers, and trucks, my newly acquired sixth sense vanished. Perhaps it was the noise, the energy level, or the death of so many. Perhaps I had grown too tired to hear them. But if we listen, animals will speak to us with their eyes, their hearts, and their souls. If we listen.

Pets roamed the empty streets searching for any morsel of food left behind. Unfortunately, anything found was no longer edible, having been saturated by some of the most polluted water on earth.

Photo: Nancy Cleveland

Chapter 14

Strays: Against All Odds

I f you look closely in your own hometown, you will see them: Strays. They make their homes on the harsh, forbidding streets in every city and town of the world. Life is cruel for them. They have nowhere to turn, no assurance of food from day to day, no secure place to sleep.

Strays: millions of thin, quivering cats and dogs that are either lost, abandoned, or born onto the streets. They slowly learn how to survive on very little. They learn their neighborhoods, the animals around them, the people who will feed them, and the dumpsters they can rummage through.

When you see these animals they are usually gazing back at you over their shoulders as they wait, poised, ready to sprint, assessing the situation, Is it safe to stay? Or safer to run? Strays. Even in a normal environment, in a bustling city with discarded food items and people all around, theirs is a difficult, short life.

On the Gulf after Katrina, it was an impossible life. Overnight the Big Easy became a city of strays. An urban hell full of lapdogs and house cats suddenly thrust onto the mean streets of an abandoned city. Pets that had lived with a family, enjoyed regular meals, a routine, had a favorite toy, a nickname, were suddenly on their own. Pets that just yesterday were coddled by their owners, used to their safe, enclosed worlds, were now alone and confused.

New Orleans became a city full of strays that didn't know how to *be* strays. Didn't know how to survive the streets. The Big Easy was a city full of lost, incapable animals. Pets with no street savvy, no ability to survive, no place to turn. Overnight New Orleans was teeming with novice roaming animals. And worse—it wasn't a normal city by any standards. There were few people. No places to rummage. No fast food stops, convenience stores, or gas stations to forage at. No safe, clean places to sleep. No friendly neighbors to care for them—there were no neighbors at all.

The animals freed from their homes were only a bit luckier than those still inside. Having escaped their wet, moldy homes, they had fresher air. And they had a *slim* chance to find food left out by volunteers or to be spotted by a rescuer. But they had little to survive on. Except for the few pet-feeding stations around town, the toxic flood saturated all pre-existing food sources, and oil, bacteria, and sewage contaminated the once fresh drinking water.

Even the most hardcore, streetwise stray from any city of the world would have quickly perished in New Orleans after Katrina. Yet miraculously, some pets survived. Many are still there, against all odds. They roam the devastated region searching for food, safety, and family.

So when you see strays in your own hometown, perhaps you will leave them some food, give them a chance, take them in; otherwise, for them it's a grim, short life. And if you are ever in New Orleans, or anywhere on the hurricane-ravaged Gulf, and you see a stray, perhaps you will leave it some food, give it a chance, take it in. For theirs is an impossible life.

"All the arguments to prove man's superiority cannot shatter this hard fact: in suffering the animals are our equals."
~Peter Singer

I WILL LOVE THE LIGHT FOR IT SHOWS ME THE WAY, YET I WILL ENDURE THE DARKNESS FOR T SHOWS ME THE STARS. -OG MANDINO

Our lives begin to end the day we become silent about things that matter.
~R. Whitney Brown

"THE GREATEST GIFT IS A PORTION OF THYSELF."
~RALPH WALDO EMERSON

"The world is a dangerous place, not because of those who do evil, but because of those who look on and do nothing."
Albert Einstein

Nobody made a greater mistake than he who did nothing because he could do only a little.
~Edmund Burke

When you are joyous, look deep into your heart and you shall find it is only that which has given you sorrow that is giving you joy. When you are sorrowful look again in your heart, and you shall see that in truth you are weeping for that which has been your delight.
~ Kahlil Gibran

Courage is going from failure to failure without losing enthusiasm.
~Winston Churchill

To ease another's heartache is to forget one's own."
~Abe Lincoln

"Most of the important things in the world have been accomplished by people who have kept on trying when there seemed to be no hope at all."
~Dale Carnegie

You become responsible forever for what you've tamed.
Ann and le Saint-Exupéry

"Until one has loved an animal, a part of one's soul remains unawakened"
~Anatole France

"I am a part of all that I have met."
~Alfred Lord Tennyson

"Think occasionally of the suffering of which you spare yourself the sight." ~Albert Schweitzer

Created by Nancy Clifford

Found with a broken tail, broken jaw, and one eye missing, this poor little guy was rescued and named One-Eyed Jack. He now lives in California.

Chapter 15

The Cat in Catastrophe

Cats were everywhere in New Orleans. Everywhere, yet nowhere to be found. They were the tragic, scared survivors hidden in cars, behind buildings, and in blistering attics. They were tucked away in treetops, behind closets, under beds. They cowered on street corners, in alleys, under highway bridges. They were the traumatized, crouching animals that no longer played joyfully or frolicked with a bounce in their step. After Katrina, cats slithered and scurried, hugging tight to the ground.

Dashing away, they would stop, hesitate a moment, and gaze back at you. Stare you in the eye as if deciding whether to stay or go. But the pause was always brief ... the answer always the same ... they would continue on their way.

Cats were the stealthy, secretive creatures that desperately needed our help and yet their suspicious, fearful nature made them their own worst enemy. They were the tragic, slight figures that often slipped though our hands and vanished from sight.

When I think of New Orleans, I will always remember the cats. How fast, how scared, how alone—and how misunderstood. While some volunteers had great sensitivity for these sweet, complex animals, others had no experience with felines. They believed that cats were survivors and could handle anything, anywhere. You know, they had all those lives to spare. For some rescuers, all their attention was on the dogs. But no animal could survive the famine after Katrina. Misunderstood, these elusive felines had everything working against them. Unlike dogs that could be heard in the distance barking, calling us to their rescue, the quiet meow of cats went unheard. These beloved pets, docile and gentle before the trauma of Katrina, now appeared to be feral—animals unfamiliar with human contact.

Hissing, scratching, and biting volunteers, they were often released back onto the streets, as we had nowhere to send them. For the overcrowded system, foster homes and shelters nationwide barely had room for their own local tame cats, let alone these "imported" aggressive "ferals."

Rescuer Kris Rieck took home thirty-three of these "vicious" cats to her sanctuary in the Carolinas. These cats would have had no other fate than to be re-released to fend for themselves on the harsh streets of New Orleans. As weeks passed, Kris would discover that only two were truly feral cats, and the rest were gentle, playful kitties that talked incessantly, loved to be petted, enjoyed chasing grasshoppers, and always won when batting toy mice around.

Yes, cats had it bad in New Orleans. And still do. Tens of thousands of tame felines and true ferals still struggle on the streets of the Gulf, with little food or water and few volunteers to help.

Please remember the cats in all catastrophes. These stealthy, secretive creatures will be there. They will be helpless and desperate for your aid.

I've struck it rich, finding a "Hello Kitty" in Chalmette, Louisiana.

Chapter 16

Hello Kitty

Ben was about thirty, skinny as a whittled twig, and a dog person. I don't know if he arrived in New Orleans that scrawny, or got that way from weeks of stress, no food, and carrying fifty-pound bags of dog food, but one thing was *certain* about Ben—he didn't "get" cats. Many people who never spent time with felines don't understand them. Growing up around canines, they're accustomed to a dog's in-your-face attitude.

Cats are slower, quieter, and a bit more cerebral. Okay, *a lot* more cerebral. While dogs are busy doing things, cats are busy thinking about them. Hence these playful, silly creatures are often misunderstood.

"What's with cats?" Ben asked. "Only one came to me for help. In three weeks, only one cat came to me."

"In three weeks?" I said. "It usually takes about a month to find a cat like that."

I called them Hello Kitties. They were there ... but they were rare. While most cats were scared to death and in flight mode, these dainty creatures would strut up with a rub on your legs and a confident greeting, "Meow, meow." And I knew exactly what they meant. They meant: "Where have you been? Why haven't I been fed? What's with all the dirty water? And how come my house is a mess?"

No matter how much tragedy swirled around them, these talkative kitties were there to remind you that things were not up to standard and that someone had better take action—preferably you—and right now. Finding the rare Hello Kitty was like winning the rescue lottery; like finding hidden treasure on a scavenger hunt of enormous proportions. I only encountered six Hello Kitties out of the thousands of starving, petrified felines that ran, terrified.

I remember breaking into a locked, water-filled house and seeing a kitten at the top of the stairs. The tiny girl came charging down the steps and jumped into my arms with one loud, definitive "Meow!" I knew exactly what she said, for it was very clear: "You call yourself a rescuer? You're late! A girl could starve waiting for you!"

Then she paused, eyed me pensively, and rubbed her face on my cheek, releasing a soft purr. "Never mind," she said. "I forgive you. Let's just go. It's way past dinnertime."

Rescuer Angela Tucker greets two lost Rottweilers on the deserted I-10 highway that cuts through New Orleans. Before Katrina, this road was bumper-to-bumper traffic. The city became a ghost town where homeless animals wandered in search of help.

Chapter 17

I'm With You

Song lyrics by Avril Lavigne and The Matrix.
© Warner, 2001

I'm standing on the bridge
I'm waiting in the dark
I thought that you'd be here by now

There's nothing but the rain
No footsteps on the ground

I'm listening, but there's no sound
Isn't anyone trying to find me?
Won't somebody come take me home?

It's a damn cold night
Trying to figure out this life
Won't you take me by the hand, take me somewhere new
I don't know who you are but I ... I'm with you
I'm with you

I'm looking for a place
I'm searching for a face
Is anybody here I know
'Cause nothing's going right and
Everything's a mess
And no one likes to be alone

Isn't anyone trying to find me?
Won't somebody take me home?
It's a damn cold night
Trying to figure out this life
Won't you take me by the hand, take me somewhere new
I don't know who you are but I, I'm with you
I'm with you

Oh, why is everything so confusing
Maybe I'm just out of my mind

It's a damn cold night
Trying to figure out this life
Won't you take me by the hand, take me somewhere new
I don't know who you are but I, I'm with you

I'm with you

Take me by the hand, take me somewhere new
I don't know who you are but I, I'm with you

I'm with you

Take me by the hand, take me somewhere new
I don't know who you are but I, I'm with you

I'm with you
I'm with you.

Chapter 18

Disaster Dan

D an was staring across the room. I couldn't tell if he was deep in thought or sleeping with his eyes open. Iguanas are hard to figure out. After about an hour of this deep stare, he moved his foot. Then I realized—why, yes—he *had* been deep in thought. The whole time he was thinking about moving his foot.

To me, that was an iguana. They crawl, they stare, they blink occasionally—and every once in a while they'll do a silly push-up just to keep you awake. It wasn't until I met Dan that my shallow opinion of reptiles changed.

We found him in the back room of a Katrina-damaged house. We didn't just find him. We didn't just stumble across him the way we did with many pets before—Dan was bequeathed to us by his owner.

A month after Katrina, a rescuer and I noticed a couple walking down a deserted street in northeast New Orleans. We asked if they had seen or heard any animals, if any of their neighbors had pets left behind or locked in houses. "Nope, not a one," said the woman.

We continued our search as the couple stepped away, surveying their devastated neighborhood. After a few minutes the woman turned back to us. "Down there at the corner house there's an iguana in the back room. It doesn't look too good. You can have it if you want it."

"We'll go look, but we'd like to get him back to his owner," I said.

"I am the owner," the woman replied.

And so began the saga of Disaster Dan. An unloved, unwanted, left-for-dead reptile that was soon to become one of the most spoiled, loved, cared about iguanas this side of the Mississippi.

Dan was whisked off to the MuttShack rescue outpost and handed to Diane Walsh for intake. He took one long, studious look at her, then crawled up her arm and onto her head. It was love at first sight for both of them.

Like me, Diane had grown up around cats and dogs. She had never spent time with an iguana and it wasn't high on her list of things to do. Like me, she agreed that they were strange, scaly creatures; toy dinosaurs that somehow snuck out of the Jurassic Period. … not too bright, not too friendly, and not too big in the personality department.

But that was the old Diane. Today's Diane can't imagine life without her iguana. "He's more human than my other pets," she informed me "He's smart, silly, playful. He loves to soak in a warm tub. Loves to sunbathe. He's a vegetarian. And always sleeps with his head on his little Santa pillow. I've discovered that iguanas keep secrets really well. Life with an iguana can change quickly."

"Change quickly?" I asked. "He had to think for an hour once just to move his foot."

Diane sent me the following e-mail:

I took Dan to Dr. Eileen today because he was losing weight. I thought he had cancer from sitting in toxic waste for a month before he was rescued.

Dr. Eileen did X-rays and it turns out Dan is pregnant.

"She" is full of eggs! She isn't eating because she is so full of eggs she feels full.

So Dan just had a $220 pregnancy test. Actually, her eggs won't hatch because they were not fertilized. There is no sign of anything at all wrong with her. I'm so relieved! I love this little guy—girl.

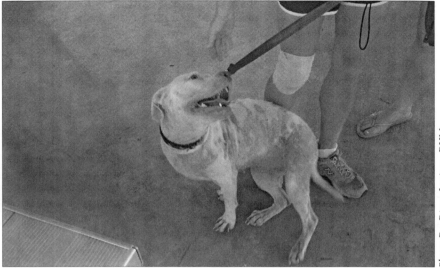

A sweet, scared pit bull, suffering from mange, is consoled by an animal rescuer.

Chapter 19

Death by Pit Bull

I always thought I'd die in a plane wreck, sitting in first class next to some celebrity who was pretending to read a screenplay so no one would bother him. Or I'd die in a car crash, hit by a Bentley driven by some celebrity pretending to read a screenplay so no one would bother him.

Instead I was staring down the muzzle of a loaded pit bull. I hate to make light of this but I've always had a problem with death, especially mine. But death by pit bull never figured into my plans, and New Orleans was a city full of pit bulls.

The "bully" breeds seemed to be the dog *du jour* in the region. In my estimation (granted, I still count on my fingers) 40 percent of all dogs rescued were pits, chows, and Rottweilers. And if there is one thing I learned about these dogs, they've gotten a bum rap. Pit bulls were among the sweetest dogs I encountered on the Gulf.

And by the way, if you think rescuing on the Gulf meant holding out a handful of pet food while doggies followed you down the street wagging their tails ... nope. It was more often a thirty-minute fight in a slippery wet, debris-filled room—a room you locked yourself in to contain any animals stuck inside. They were alone. They were scared. They were traumatized—and you just broke into *their* house. The truth is, rescuing was a very dangerous job. Some Gulf volunteers, inexperienced with aggressive animals, were mauled or permanently scarred by panicked dogs. I went with one rescuer to the military ship the *Iwo Jima* for plastic surgery to have his cheek sewn back on. Vicious cat bites were all too common and often required a rescuer's hospitalization ... including mine, twice.

So there I was, locked in the back room with yet another confused, angry dog. I was upstairs in an apartment weeks after Katrina hit. Which meant this scrawny pit bull was close to death and, I guessed, wanted company on the trip. He was definitely out for blood. But then I noticed something; he wasn't *really* out for blood. He was out for ... water.

Every time I approached his corner, he lunged. Often, aggressive dogs are a lot more equal opportunity. They will attack equally, at any opportunity, but it was obvious that this dog just didn't want me near his corner. Then I noticed, behind him, gallon jugs of water. His private stash. Thick, sturdy plastic bottles with blue handles and impossible-to-open lids. The kind of stubborn, hard lids that scrape the skin off your palm as you struggle to unscrew them. Bottles this dog had dragged to his corner from all over the apartment. Bottles he was trying desperately to open. The heavy plastic tops were all chewed at, but none had opened. This pit bull was guarding his looted property. He realized that he needed the water inside and had been trying for weeks to get at it. Then I show up—uninvited. No way was he sharing.

I grew to love pits after working with them in New Orleans. Most were gentle animals that wanted affection. But we all met those that were *really* out for blood. They'd been trained to be that way, victims of their owners, taught everything they knew by the real bully breeds—the cruel, ignorant, heartless humans who had used them as pawns in their abusive, sick games. We all met the pits that were trained to hate, to attack, to kill. And sadder still, the pits that were scarred from head to toe; the loving, gentle creatures used as "bait," thrown unwillingly into dogfights so that the more aggressive pits could practice their deadly skills.

There I was, with the dehydrated pit bull locked in the back room. Finally I wrangled a bottle of water from him and wrenched the top open. We sat down together and shared it. I opened, he drank—two gallons nonstop.

Animals tried to chew open water jugs.

And the good news: it wasn't my time to go. My life would not end there with death by pit bull. I'd still have a chance to die in a plane, in first class, sitting next to some celebrity pretending to read a screenplay so no one would bother him. Or die in a car wreck, hit by a Bentley, driven by some celebrity pretending to read a screenplay so no one would bother him. What a relief.

We Can Make a Difference

Many pet owners left their tub water dripping and toilet seats up for their pets to access water. In a catastrophe, pipes break and sewers back up. In New Orleans, water was undrinkable, contaminated with bacteria, and thick with sewage. If you must leave a pet behind, leave containers of fresh water everywhere. Pets can only last a few days without water.

Chapter 20

One Lucky Dog

The dog was confined inside a splintered, peeling tool shed hidden off the road behind the main house. He had been locked inside the sweltering, ten-foot-by-ten-foot tomb for six weeks. And he was locked in tight. A heavy deadbolt made sure nothing could get in … or out.

With no food, water, stimulus, or human contact, he was on death row and his time was up. But he wasn't going down without a fight. The dog had chewed and scratched a hole in the bottom of

85

the wooden door, creating a jagged window, his only contact with the bleak world outside.

Call it fate, happenstance, destiny, luck, or divine intervention, but many animals on the Gulf were saved by complete accident. I had gotten lost and found a beagle stranded at the docks. Made a wrong turn and found a mother cat and her kittens in the garbage. Went to the wrong address and found a rabbit stuck in a cage on a kitchen table. On the Gulf there were no wrong addresses, no wrong turns, no accidents.

Weeks after Katrina, the blistering heat teamed up with the fog-thick humidity to take its toll on everyone. Rescuer Nancy Cleveland and I were exhausted, late in the day, as we cut through a neighborhood. Always on the lookout for stranded pets, we spotted a skeletal cat inside a house; she meowed to us frantically from the upstairs window. She paced back and forth in the window screaming to us, but with the thick glass, we couldn't hear her.

I ran to the back of the house to see if there were any easy entry points. As I moved up the driveway, something caught my eye. To the right something moved. And there he was, in the backyard next door, peering out at me, his sorrowful eyes speaking to me.

If we hadn't been driving down that street at that moment ... if the cat hadn't been in the window that second ... if the dog hadn't been peeking out his opening to the world that instant ... he would have died right there, alone, in that splintered, peeling tool shed hidden off the road behind the main house. He was one lucky dog.

We Can Make a Difference

If you must leave your pet behind, mark your house well with permanent markers or waterproof paint. Make sure the message is big enough to be visible from the street and never leave the writing on breakable windows. Here is a sample of a great message. This was the only house I found in New Orleans that showed us the status of the pets.

Photo: KO

The owners boarded up their house making it clear to all that there were no pets inside.

A Survivor Speaks...

Photo: Jocelyn Augustino/FEMA

Chapter 21

Hi, My Name Is Nicole Will, and Me and My Family Were There for Katrina

n Nicole's words, this is her story: 8/29/2005 was the day Katrina came on shore to my parish (St. Bernard Parish). It was me, my husband, my mother-in-law, my father-in-law, my seven-year-old son, my two-year-old son, my one-year-old daughter, and my pit bull Papa. At the time I was nine months along and due any day to have my second little girl.

We watched at my front door as Katrina made her way picking up trees, parts of the roofs, carports, and just tossing everything around. Everyone was awake for Katrina, it was about 11:00 a.m. when we all went to sleep. My two sons stayed up and were playing in the bedroom. Then my oldest son went to my mother-in-law's room and told her that the house was flooding. She got up to see her feet under the water. By the time she got from her room to mine the water was up to her knees. My one-year-old was in her playpen at the time and was floating on top of the water around my room. I grabbed her before she went under the water.

My husband was in the attic trying to get a hole in the roof, but he couldn't break through with the hammer. When he came down from the attic, my toddler was crying and screaming. My husband and father-in-law got my icebox that was floating out of the kitchen into the living room. They emptied out the food and the other things that were in it and put pillows from my sofa that was floating around the living room inside the icebox, then put my two sons inside of it. My dog was in my bedroom floating on top of my bed being a good little boy. Now chest deep in the water, we had no way out of the house.

My husband remembers we had a shotgun on top of the shelf in the closet. He went to get it out and came back to start shooting the roof. We finally get out of the house to the roof. My husband was the first up there, then my mother-in-law, my kids, then my dog, then me. Last but not least my father-in-law. We got into my friend's boat but it wouldn't start so we was pushed seven houses away from mine. My husband and father-in-law got us to the roof of some other home; while we stayed in the boat they were trying to get to another boat.

That's when I heard my husband yell out, "Is everything okay?"

I replied, "We're sinking."

By the time he got to us I handed him our infant; as soon as my fingers left her side the boat flipped over on us. Me and my seven–year-old were in the water. I pushed him up to the rope and he pulled himself out of the water. My mother-in-law and my toddler were under the boat. She popped up out of the water without my son so I went to look for him. I found him under the boat trying his hardest to stay on top the water, so I took him by the waist and got him to the roof. At that time I was so tired I couldn't swim anymore. I started to drown, then my husband jumped in after me and pulled me by the hair to the top of a blue van. That's how I got on the roof.

My dog, named Papa, was already up there when I got there. We stayed on the roof for about five hours until someone came in his boat to get us and bring us to St. Bernard High School where me, my mother-in-law, and kids stayed for a day and a half. Then the Coast Guards came in helicopters and got all the elderly and sick first, then all women and children. I lost all contact with my husband and dog for about seven days. When we got to Texas, at the hotel, my aunt posted me and my family on MSNBC. That's where my husband found us and called my aunt's house around 3:00 a.m. She gave him our room phone number and he called us. Two days later he was back with us but had no dog with him. I asked where he was; he told me that he left him in the school with a note around his neck with all his information on the note.

—Nicole Will

Beside the name and address of the family, the note also included this cryptic message:

PAPA
PLEASE DO NOT SHOOT
VERY FRENDLY DOG

When Nicole and all survivors were forced to evacuate the school, she overheard a sheriff state that when the owners left he was going to "shoot all the animals and chop them up for crab bait." She spread the word among evacuees. No one believed it would really happen, yet nervous survivors left notes on walls and attached to their pets, begging authorities not to shoot them. Hence the note above that was hanging from Papa's neck includes: *PLEASE DO NOT SHOOT.*

But Nicole's greatest fear came true. Papa was among the

thirty-two pets killed soon after the families evacuated the school. All pets were shot multiple times, executed at close range. St. Bernard High wasn't the only pet massacre case in that parish. Displaced residents who gathered at three other schools were also forced to evacuate and entrust their pets to others. All of these schools became shooting ranges for survivors' harmless pets.

As rescuers in the area, we all heard rumors about officers shooting strays and killing dogs found guarding their destroyed homes. Sheriff Mike Milton was caught red-handed shooting strays on the streets when Dallas Morning News photojournalist David Leeson videotaped Minton shooting—and dead dogs nearby. In an interview Minton stated, "This is really better for that dog. Where's he gonna find food? It's more humane for that dog—"

The reporter asks: "So how many dogs?"

"Enough," Minton said as he looked away and laughed.

For two years the case lumbered through the Louisiana court system but in the end all charges against former deputy sheriff Mike Minton and Sergeant Clifford "Chip" Englande were dismissed, owing to lack of substantial evidence. Even though the reporter saw the shooting, heard the gun, saw a dog drop, and even though he filmed glimpses of the events, the bullet was not seen entering the dog; hence it could not be proven that Milton caused the death. In addition, to the disappointment of the Attorney General's office, residents did not step forward to pursue their claims against the street shootings, both for fear of the local sheriffs and because they had no emotional reserve to suffer through the painful court case. Although the case of street shootings was dismissed against Milton and Englande, the pet shootings at the St. Bernard schools are still under investigation. If you or anyone you know has information, please contact the Louisiana Attorney General's office.

As Papa's body was never recovered in the carnage at the high school, Nicole still searches the Internet and all leads to find her "baby boy."

This lucky umbrella cockatoo came in without its home address. An all white bird, almost impossible to distinguish from other cockatoos, he was reunited when his owner was able to describe the cage.

Chapter 22

Without a Trace

S he told me she became a vet first, then switched careers to become a lawyer—an advocate for animals. She said she was from Arkansas and her husband was a dog whisperer. Her name was Tammy. Tammy Hanson. She would show up at the Winn-Dixie parking lot from time to time in her black SUV. We were glad to see her—she would take the bigger dogs back to Arkansas to foster them. She'd fill her truck with "bullies," the aggressive and hard-to-handle dogs. It was always a relief to see Tammy; we desperately needed to move these pets.

It was hard for us. With so few people there at first you had to make a decision—stay and walk the dogs and keep the pet cages clean, or search for the animals waiting for you, relying on you, left alone behind locked doors. We'd be up early trying to care for the animals, then race out into the city. Some people stayed behind—they preferred to work with the rescued pets—while others didn't. I never stayed behind. I always rescued. I knew the areas we'd been in, the areas still untouched. I felt a responsibility to go out, just as others felt a responsibility to stay and care for the animals already saved.

It all needed to be done. But stay or go, with so little help and so few supplies, it was a lose-lose situation all around. There was no way to win in New Orleans. Tammy wasn't the only one who came to "help" us at Winn-Dixie. A white van would appear, painted with parrots and a wildlife sanctuary logo on the side. They were often there when I came in to drop off rescued pets. They took the big parrots and exotic animals. As exhausted rescuers, we were glad when the experts showed up.

I don't know where these experts came from, how they found us, or where they went when they left us, but I knew someone had contacted them and they were dedicated enough to carry the animals to safety.

Or so it seemed.

One of the many harsh truths in New Orleans is that these animals will never be seen again. They vanished without a trace. Stolen for a myriad of reasons. I would later discover that some of those beautiful birds were worth thousands each. They would be sold all over the USA. Like stolen gems, this was a Katrina black market, impossible to track. Avian veterinarian, Dr. Julie Burge, who came to assist in Louisiana, states: "Many Katrina birds that were rescued will never be found by their owners. After the hard work the rescuers did finding these animals and getting them to safety, people showed up at the shelters and triage centers like

Winn-Dixie, claiming to be bird sanctuaries, and took truckloads of birds away. Most of these birds were never listed on Petfinders, and were likely sold in other states. I have reports from rescue workers who said they were grateful that someone who knew about birds was going to take care of them as they were swamped with dogs and cats to care for. They had no idea anyone would stoop so low as to steal the pets that may have been the only thing some of these evacuees had left."

And Tammy Hanson? She was no vet. She was no lawyer. She was a hoarder, a serial dog collector. She took truckloads of traumatized, innocent pit bulls and Rottweilers to their new home in Arkansas on acres of wooded land, where they would live outdoors with no shelter, tucked away in small cages alongside hundreds of other trapped dogs. Many would die there. I will never be free of the guilt of handing Tammy my rescued pets. Dogs that had already suffered so much were now given another death sentence.

The truth about Tammy was discovered in mid-October when a volunteer who helped at her farm, where there were more than 600 dogs on the property, turned her in. Tammy was pursued by local Sheriff Montgomery and charged with 28 counts of animal abuse in Baxter County, Arkansas, in a case dubbed "Barkansas". Tammy disappeared before sentencing and was later found guilty in July of 2007 in Vermont.

The Hansons had been living in Vermont under assumed names—Christine and Henry Miller—when the Montgomery police got a tip that Christine Miller was in fact Tammy Hanson. She and her husband were arrested and brought back to Arkansas for trial.

New Orleans was lose-lose, no matter how hard you tried. There was simply no way to win in the Big Easy.

We Can Make a Difference

Anyone taking pets from a disaster zone must leave copies of the driver's licenses of all people in the vehicle. They should sign and date a paper listing the number and types of animals taken. A photo of their vehicle, showing their license plate, should be kept with the paperwork, along with photos of the animals removed.

Even today, animal stealing is a rampant multi-million dollar industry all over America. Class B dealers make a fortune selling our adored pets to research labs. These Class B or "random source" dealers regularly buy dogs from auctions, flea markets, or "shelters." (Using the word "shelter" implies they are safe havens or "shelters" rather than the concrete warehouses they *really* are, where more than six million innocent pets will be destroyed yearly in the USA.) While a few pounds have finally gone no-kill and others do care about the pets and try their best to save them, far too many are an inhumane end-of-the-road for the animals that step inside their doors. When a rescuer complained to one pound in Kentucky that they were not feeding their animals, the manager told her: "Why should we waste the food, we're gonna kill them anyway. Why bother?"

Class B dealers also buy pets from "bunchers," people who collect animals from random sources. Class B dealers and bunchers have been known to snag lost, stray, or free-to-a-good-home pets. Pets are also stolen from cars, outside shops, and from their own backyards.

One former commercial dog trader from the Midwest admitted that many of the dogs sold to research were clearly people's pets. "Mostly hounds, gentle animals, house dogs, or pets. Y'know, something that wouldn't bite you. They had collars with their name on them." The trader went on to explain that dogs would come from several states and that the people selling the dogs would write down fake names and addresses for the dogs, creating a phony paper trail.

Never give your pet away unless you know for sure where it's going. Free-to-good-home ads on Craigslist and in newspapers are monitored by bunchers looking for free pets to sell for profit. Bunchers have been known to answer ads with children in tow to help them appear to be legitimate pet owners and family people. If you must give a pet away, ask the interested party for the name of their vet. It's easy enough to check out how they care for animals.

Be extra careful if you live in Oklahoma or Minnesota. Both states have pound seizure laws. Over the years, thousands of pets have been sold or given to laboratories for research, as both states have laws that *require* government-run pounds to surrender animals to any licensed research institutions that request them. While *many* states once adhered to pound seizure laws, Utah was also one of the last three states that were mandated to give up their pound pets for experimentation. Fortunately, in March of 2010, Utah changed this law and they no longer give their pets to research facilities. (Don't be fooled – although most states are no longer obligated *by law* to hand over pets, many states still sell their pets to labs. It's their choice.) For further info on the regulations of Oklahoma and Minnesota, as well as the rules of *your* own state, read the story: "What's Happening in *Your* Local Pound?" in the resources section at the end of this book.

Photo: Jocelyn Augustino/FEMA

Chapter 23

THE WEB

Man's Best Friend: ~~A Dog~~

Ette Unger saved three starving kittens from the Manor Apartments on Johnson Street in New Orleans without stepping foot in that neighborhood. She had never even been to New Orleans. Ette rescued the kitties from five thousand miles away—in Dublin, Ireland.

They say man's best friend is a dog, but after Katrina the Web ran a close second place. In cyberspace, animal rescuers all over the Gulf teamed up with animal rescuers all over the globe to trade information, raise funds, arrange to ship goods, and get updates on pets left behind.

Ette explained: "Even though I live in Ireland, I have always had affection for New Orleans, so when I heard Katrina was approaching, I watched with dread. I kept up on the Internet through online news sources, forums, and posts on Craigslist and a New Orleans-based group—Nola.com.

"The first time I visited Nola.com was a few days before the hurricane. While some people were rushing to evacuate the city, others were heading for the Superdome. Online, I read an article in the *Times-Picayune* newspaper and it stayed in my mind. A man in his twenties arrived at the Superdome with his kitten. He was stopped at the entrance and told he couldn't take his pet inside. 'She's only a nine-month-old kitten,' he said. 'How could she survive outside in a hurricane?' Denied admittance to the Superdome, he left to ride out the storm.

"As the story of Katrina and the floods played out on international news," Ette remembered, "I used the Internet to see if I could help somehow. To my amazement, evacuees were posting desperate messages to rescuers to save the pets left behind, pets locked in their homes."

While owners frantically searched for help on the Web, others en route to New Orleans tracked their messages and made lists of owners' addresses. With no electricity in the city, and no time for rescuers to sit on battery-charged computers all day, they needed outside help, phone calls made, research done. Internet volunteers became a fast conduit, spending hours on the Web daily to filter information back and forth from evacuated pet owners to rescuers on the ground.

The Internet was worked to the bone before, during, and after Katrina. Rescued pets were sent to foster homes and shelters nationwide, either with no paperwork or with a trail of paperwork that *didn't* work. With the enormity of the disaster, the lack of volunteers, and the makeshift system to document animals, many owners would never see their pets again. This led to the creation of still more Internet assistants and reunion groups such as the Stealth Volunteers. Sifting through the maze of confusing paperwork and contacting thousands of shelters and foster homes throughout the United States, this grassroots army of researchers worked full time to help reunite lost pets with their owners.

In the aftermath of Hurricane Katrina, the Internet was one of the best networking tools available. For Ette, it led to many contacts and resources, which enabled her to save the lives of the three starving kittens.

In Dublin, Ette was on the Internet reading *The Times-Picayune*, where a reporter had written about a resident who refused to leave his apartment as he *"promised his neighbors, the ones who escaped from the roof by helicopter after Katrina, that he would protect the stuffed backpacks and suitcases they could not carry with them to safety."* Special agents were unable to convince the man to evacuate and instead left plenty of provisions and scheduled return trips to check on him. But as Ette read further the article stated: *"He and another man were the lone holdouts in a dark building, where starving kittens prowled hallways strewn with soiled T-shirts and children's toys."*

Starving kittens? Ette contacted the newspaper reporter and was able to get the apartment's address. Posting everywhere to find rescuers with the time to go there, others on the Internet joined her plight, including Rosemary S. from Sydney, Australia, a mother in Alaska, and Americans from all over the United States. With non-stop emergencies, problems with communication, and a lack of volunteers, it took three weeks and Internet volunteers on three continents to coordinate the rescue of the starving kittens.

Thanks to the World Wide Web, America's biggest national disaster was aided by an international relief effort. For animal rescue, the Web was—and is—man's best friend. Or at least runs a close second. Woof.

The silent scream.

Chapter 24

City of Sorrow

For every story told there are thousands of stories just as tragic, desperate, sad, and unique; tales that will never be told. It is my greatest fear that whenever I document a life, or death, that we may forget the untold others. But I cannot tell their stories. Their last moments were unseen ... their desperate cries unheard ... their final struggles unknown. I can only hope that by focusing on a few that the rest will live in the hearts and minds of all of us.

Photo: Dana Kay Deutsch

Deadly heartworms and other diseases were commonly found in rescued Gulf pets. These are two of a family of four rescued chihuahuas. The little tan girl needed heart surgery to remove the spaghetti-length worms causing congestive heart failure.

Vets I've spoken to nationwide are concerned about the heartworms Katrina pets brought with them from the Gulf. Veterinarian Debbie Cottrell, herself a volunteer in New Orleans, explained: "When they {dogs} went to their new homes, they took their heartworms with them, and in many cases spread them around their new environment via the mosquitoes there. That's why there's a lot of controversy about lawsuits of New Orleans' residents trying to get their pets back from foster homes and adopters. Many people fostering these dogs were angry, as so many of these pets had heartworm disease. That means their previous owners were not being responsible owners. These dogs came from a heartworm intense area and were not on heartworm prevention."

We Can Make a Difference

No matter where in the U.S. you live, protect your dog with heartworm medication, which comes in the form of a doggie treat and is given once a month. For this small investment, approximately thirty dollars a year, you'll help your pet live a long, healthy life.

Photo: Jocelyn Augustino/FEMA

Chapter 25

A Survivor's Tale: Eyewitness...

By Linda Walker, Survivor

All survivors have a painful story. When I was rescued, the first place I was taken to was the I-10 near Causeway Boulevard in Metairie. We were told buses would be coming to take us out of town.

There were 5,000 people, all of semi-mob mentality, with no place to sit, pushing and screaming. Finally, when I had managed to get close enough to the bus to see people two rows ahead getting on that bus, I saw a man and wife and a beautiful little wire-haired dachshund.

The woman was holding that dog, and when she was ready to board the bus the guard told her she would have to put the dog down—that she could not take him on the bus. She pleaded with the guard, the whole time clutching onto the little dog that was, of course, oblivious to what was happening. All he knew was he was being held by his mama and you could tell how happy he was.

I remember thinking at the time, *Well, at least my dog Timmy and the cats are in the apartment and I do not have to abandon them in the hot sun on a highway!* The pleading with the guard went on; the husband began pleading also but to no avail. Now the woman was sobbing and clutching that little dog to her and the little dog—still quite happy but now concerned for his owner, who he realized was sad—started licking her face as the tears streamed down. He just wanted to lick those tears away so she would not be sad anymore. She began to beg again and then she seemed to indicate to her husband that she would get on the bus, but they tried then to get the guard or someone to take the dog so they would not have to just let him loose in that madhouse alone.

I do not know what happened because at that moment God, in his infinite goodness, allowed me to have a mild asthma attack so I would not have to watch the rest of that awful story play out, and I was escorted to a makeshift med area on the neutral ground. I have thought of that little dog and those people so many times and hope the animal survived and that somehow they were once again reunited. That little dog showed such fierce love for that woman and was so joyful to be in her arms and wanted to just lick all her tears away.

We Can Make a Difference

Your plan must be ready in case of impending disasters. Have cages, leashes, food, and any medicines available. Put photos of your pets and copies of their paperwork in no-leak plastic bags. If you have larger animals like horses, goats, or pigs, have a list of friends, neighbors, and rescue groups with trailers to help you evacuate. Plan today, early, not once a disaster is en route. Always have current ID tags on your pets at all times. Far too many Gulf pets had no collars and tags. This is what led to most pets being lost in the system. An ID tag, whether your pet is in a disaster zone or not, may be your animal's only chance of finding you again. More than 80 percent of pets lost nationwide without ID will never return home.

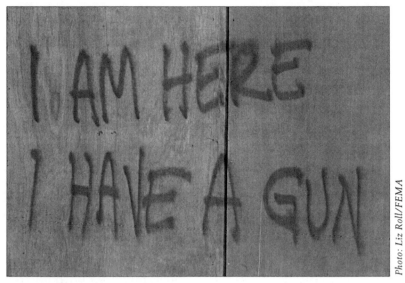

Photo: Liz Roll/FEMA

Gulf residents had a simple message for potential looters.

Chapter 26

Looting the Looters

No question, New Orleans was a dangerous, deadly city after Katrina, and what would seem crazy anywhere else on earth was accepted as almost the norm here. Like looting. If you thought TV's *Survivor, Treasure Hunt,* or *The Amazing Race* were interesting reality shows, you would have loved the most exciting reality game of all, New Orleans' own *Looting the Looters.*

Here's how it worked: The object was to empty the looters' dens before the looters emptied their guns into you. How you did it was your choice. No rule books. No instructions. No maps telling you where to hunt. Not even clues. You were completely on your own.

105

Looting the Looters was a fast paced game of luck, chance, irony, and the essential ingredient—danger.

Participants could be any age, gender, weight, height, or nationality. The only criterion for players was a touch of insanity, the ability to dodge bullets, and the strength to carry large amounts of stolen items while running for your life. The only rule to *Looting the Looters* was that you could not actively search for dens—the game would only begin if you stumbled upon a den while searching day and night for animals. Any rescuer who could find a minute to play games on the Gulf was disqualified and would have been killed by fellow rescuers, if they hadn't died of guilt first.

Unlike television, the prizes in New Orleans weren't millions of dollars. Anyone able to loot a looter was awarded with all the dry footwear, jeans, baseball caps, and flashlights they could carry.

You must play to win. If you lose, no one will ever know what happened to you, but if you succeed you'll be the hit of the rescue camp. As rescuers, we worked day and night in tarry mud, moldy debris, and toxic water. With no way to clean clothes, we wore the same mud-sodden garments and wet boots everyday. A pair of clean socks, fresh jeans, and dry footwear were the most valuable items of all.

I played *Looting the Looters* three times, stumbling upon three dens: one was on the top floor of a condo complex; one was upstairs along the back wing of a motel; and the other was in the manager's office of an apartment building. You never knew whether the looters were coming back or had already left town, but you could always tell the moment you entered a den. (This is *essential* to winning the game. The sooner you realized you were in a looter's den, the faster you had to move. We're talking—run!)

While most citizens of New Orleans who stayed during Katrina stockpiled survival goods such as candles, flashlights, canned food, and water, looters had their own idea of emergency goods.

For looters, essentials for surviving a deadly hurricane were piles of new jeans (the plastic security tags still attached), boxes of unopened sneakers, stacks of baseball caps, and of course, cases of Heineken. Looters everywhere seemed to agree that a few hundred unopened CDs and DVDs would help them through any storm.

Why would anyone loot the looters? Because we desperately needed what they had. The clean, the dry, the available. I never met a rescuer who would take a thing from the citizens of the Gulf, but no one minded re-stealing from a thief with stolen property.

I was great at *Looting the Looters* because I had that one essential ingredient that all game winners had—a touch of insanity. That, and boy was I good at running while balancing a stack of boxed sneakers.

Chapter 27

Where the Wild Things Are

S
o much attention was focused on the plight of the domestic
animals left behind that it was easy to miss the wildlife struggling, often hidden, all around us.

There were deer; their silent eyes sparked to us from the
night woods as our cars sped down deserted roads. There were
raccoons foraging through empty bags at feeding stations, their
sweet masked eyes summoning us, begging us for help. Armadillos,
squirrels, mice, beavers, opossums skunks, groundhogs, birds—
their newborns drowned, their breeding grounds destroyed, their
food and water sources obliterated.

A week after Katrina I pulled into the entrance of a six-story
brick hospital, a New Orleans nursing home. The parking lot was

108

packed with cars, dozens of autos neatly arranged as if business was up and running. Yet the property had been abandoned days before. The thriving hospital was now a vacant shell; the cars, parked so carefully, would all have to be towed away. With flood lines up to their roofs, not one was operable.

Then the ducks appeared. Waddling out from behind the building, a sorry string of thin, weak birds. Spotting me, their step quickened. They began a panicked quack. An odd communication amongst themselves—and with me. Next they ran to me and finally took flight, a low, long-winged flutter over the pavement, a tired glide to reach me. Engulfing me, they were talking, squawking, quacking, clamoring, shouting for help. They devoured the bag of cat food I dumped onto the pavement.

Looking up, I noticed a pond behind the building. I approached to discover two park benches nestled up to the water's edge. Two park benches where the patients would gather to feed these feathered friends. This once picturesque pond was now a sludge-filled dump with thumb-sized silver fish, arched, dead, dotting the black tar surface. Nothing left for these treasured ducks to eat or drink. I glanced back at the flock, desperate to find every broken morsel of cat food. I eyed them carefully, individually. I was *sure* all of these birds had been given names.

As I stepped back to the entrance of the hospital, the ducks surrounded me, spoke to me in hushed tones: a thank you, an offer to stay, an invitation to return. I watched as they waddled back to the benches to wait for those familiar faces, the elderly friends who had taken care of them for years. Friends they would never see again.

Hurricane Katrina was devastating to the wildlife on the Gulf. Breeding grounds for marine mammals, turtles, fish, pelicans, and many migratory birds were eradicated. The habitats of sea turtles, Mississippi sandhill cranes, woodpeckers, and Alabama beach mice were destroyed, along with the habitats of innumerable other species. Sixteen National Wildlife Refuges were shut down. The soil contamination, destruction of vegetation, and coastal erosion will have far-reaching, detrimental effects on the future of many species in the Gulf.

In New Orleans, the poisoned floodwater contained a mix of raw sewage, bacteria, heavy metals, pesticides, chemicals, and more than six million gallons of oil. It took forty-three days, working nonstop, to pump this contaminated water into the once pristine Lake Pontchartrain. A decision, scientists agree, that will have long-lasting repercussions on the fish and birds of the area.

And the ducks at the nursing home? I left them buckets of fresh water and dumped out bags of dry cat food. I never returned to see them. I was whisked off by other tragedies, other heartbreak.

For these ducks I would never be a familiar face with the time to lounge on a bench and lovingly toss them food. I would never be a familiar face who knew their individual names. Perhaps no one ever would again.

Photo: KO

The ducks devour a pile of dry cat food.

The calm inside the storm: a pilot's view of the inner eye-wall of a Category 5 Katrina.

Chapter 28

Katrina 101

The day before Katrina hit, the National Ocean and Atmospheric Adminstration (NOAA) issued this official "inland hurricane warning" describing the impending catastrophic damage expected:

WWUS74 KLIX 281550

NPWLIX

URGENT—WEATHER MESSAGE

NATIONAL WEATHER SERVICE NEW ORLEANS LA

1011 AM CDT SUN AUG 28 2005

...DEVASTATING DAMAGE EXPECTED...

HURRICANE KATRINA...A MOST POWERFUL HURRICANE WITH UNPRECEDENTED STRENGTH...RIVALING THE INTENSITY OF HURRICANE CAMILLE OF 1969.

MOST OF THE AREA WILL BE UNINHABITABLE FOR WEEKS...PERHAPS LONGER. AT LEAST ONE HALF OF WELL-CONSTRUCTED HOMES WILL HAVE ROOF AND WALL FAILURE. ALL GABLED ROOFS WILL FAIL...LEAVING THOSE HOMES SEVERELY DAMAGED OR DESTROYED.

THE MAJORITY OF INDUSTRIAL BUILDINGS WILL BECOME NON FUNC-TIONAL. PARTIAL TO COMPLETE WALL AND ROOF FAILURE IS EXPECTED. ALL WOOD FRAMED LOW RISING APARTMENT BUILDINGS WILL BE DESTROYED. CONCRETE BLOCK LOW RISE APARTMENTS WILL SUSTAIN MAJOR DAMAGE...INCLUDING SOME WALL AND ROOF FAILURE.

HIGH RISE OFFICE AND APARTMENT BUILDINGS WILL SWAY DANGEROUSLY...A FEW TO THE POINT OF TOTAL COLLAPSE. ALL WINDOWS WILL BLOW OUT.

AIRBORNE DEBRIS WILL BE WIDESPREAD...AND MAY INCLUDE HEAVY ITEMS SUCH AS HOUSEHOLD APPLIANCES AND EVEN LIGHT VEHICLES. SPORT UTILITY VEHICLES AND LIGHT TRUCKS WILL BE MOVED. THE BLOWN DEBRIS WILL CREATE ADDITIONAL DESTRUCTION. PERSONS... PETS...AND LIVESTOCK EXPOSED TO THE WINDS WILL FACE CERTAIN DEATH IF STRUCK.

POWER OUTAGES WILL LAST FOR WEEKS...AS MOST POWER POLES WILL BE DOWN AND TRANSFORMERS DESTROYED. WATER SHORTAGES WILL MAKE HUMAN SUFFERING INCREDIBLE BY MODERN STANDARDS.

THE VAST MAJORITY OF NATIVE TREES WILL BE SNAPPED OR UPROOTED. ONLY THE HEARTIEST WILL REMAIN STANDING... BUT BE TOTALLY DEFOLIATED. FEW CROPS WILL REMAIN. LIVESTOCK LEFT EXPOSED TO THE WINDS WILL BE KILLED.

AN INLAND HURRICANE WIND WARNING IS ISSUED WHEN SUSTAINED WINDS NEAR HURRICANE FORCE...OR FREQUENT GUSTS AT OR ABOVE HURRICANE FORCE...ARE CERTAIN WITHIN THE NEXT 12 TO 24 HOURS.

ONCE TROPICAL STORM AND HURRICANE FORCE WINDS ONSET...DO NOT VENTURE OUTSIDE!

Katrina, like all hurricanes, was a type of tropical cyclone, the generic term for a low- pressure system that generally forms in the tropics. A typical cyclone is accompanied by thunderstorms and, in the Northern Hemisphere, is characterized by a counterclockwise circulation of winds near the earth's surface.

Katrina landed dead center in the Atlantic hurricane season, which lasts from June to November, with the peak season from mid-August to late October.

Hurricanes are classified into five categories based on their wind speed, central pressure, and damage potential (see chart). Category 3 storms and higher are considered major hurricanes, though Categories 1 and 2 are still dangerous. Katrina reached Category 5 status in the Gulf but simmered down to a Category 3 storm over New Orleans.

Determining Hurricane Categories

Saffir-Simpson Hurricane Scale			
Scale Number (Category)	Sustained Winds (MPH)	Damage	Storm Surge
1	74-95	Minimal: Unanchored mobile homes, vegetation and signs.	4-5 feet
2	96-110	Moderate: All mobile homes, roofs, small crafts, flooding.	6-8 feet
3	111-130	Extensive: Small buildings, low-lying roads cut off.	9-12 feet
4	131-155	Extreme: Roofs destroyed, trees down, roads cut off, mobile homes destroyed. Beach homes flooded.	13-18 feet
5	More than 155	Catastrophic: Most buildings destroyed. Vegetation destroyed. Major roads cut off. Homes flooded.	Greater than 18 feet

Katrina Facts:

Since 1953, Atlantic tropical storms have been named from lists originated by the National Hurricane Center and are now maintained and updated by an international committee of the World Meteorological Organization. The lists featured only women's names until 1979. After that, men's and women's names alternated. Six lists are used in rotation. Thus, the 2001 lists were used again in 2007. The only time there is a change in the list is when a storm is so deadly or costly that the continued use of the name would be inappropriate for reasons of sensitivity. When this occurs, the name is stricken from the list and another name is selected to replace it. A hurricane named Katrina will never be seen again.

The terrorist attacks of 9/11 devastated sixty square acres in Manhattan. Katrina devastated 93,000 square miles of the Gulf Coast.

Hurricanes can produce widespread torrential rains with deadly results. Between 1970 and 1999, more people lost their lives from freshwater inland flooding associated with landfalling tropical cyclones than from any other hazard related to tropical cyclones.

Katrina was the costliest and one of the deadliest hurricanes in the history of the United States. It was the sixth strongest Atlantic hurricane ever recorded and the third strongest landfalling U.S. hurricane on record.

Forming over the Bahamas on August 23, 2005, Katrina crossed southern Florida as a moderate Category 1 hurricane, causing some deaths and flooding before strengthening rapidly in the Gulf of Mexico—becoming one of the strongest hurricanes ever recorded while at sea. The storm weakened before making its second and third landfalls as a Category 3 hurricane the morning of August 29, in southeast Louisiana and at the Louisiana/Mississippi state line. Due to its sheer size, Katrina devastated the coast as far as one hundred miles around the storm's center. She was the third major hurricane and second hurricane to reach Category 5 status in the 2005 Atlantic season.

At least 1,836 people lost their lives to Katrina and the subsequent floods, making it the deadliest U.S. hurricane since the 1928 Okeechobee hurricane. Katrina was responsible for more than $85 billion in damage. In 2005, she was said to be the costliest natural disaster in American history. However, it took two years before it was proven that the levee damage, attributed to Katrina, was actually the fault of the U.S. Army Corps of Engineers (USACE). Sandy Rosenthal, founder of Levee.org states: "The flooding in New Orleans was not a natural disaster. It was a civil engineering disaster, the worst in US history." Experts agree stating the failure of the levee system was rivaled only by the Chernobyl reactor meltdown."

Photo: Jocelyn Augustino/FEMA

An Industrial Canal breach flooded the Ninth Ward and surrounding neighborhoods.

Chapter 29

A Look at the Levees

Katrina weakened to a Category 3 storm before hitting New Orleans yet still caused failures of the levees and flood walls protecting the city and surrounding communities. Some failures were due to pressure caving in canal walls, while other breaches resulted from water overtopping the flood walls, or from the waters removing dirt under the levees, causing loss of stability.

When Katrina hit New Orleans with her weakened western wall, winds in the New Orleans area were at a Category 3 range. The storm surge from Lake Pontchartrain did not overtop the canal flood walls, as was originally believed.

Engineering experts agree that the canal walls were designed and built using substandard engineering techniques. Even when this situation became known to the USACE, they did nothing about it. Then, on August 29, flood walls and levees catastrophically failed throughout the metro area. Both the 17th Street Canal and London Canal collapsed well below design thresholds. The Industrial Canal collapsed after a brief period of overtopping caused by "scouring" or erosion of the earthen levee walls—an egregious design flaw.

This group of canals and flood walls, called the Mississippi River Gulf Outlet, breached in at least twenty places, flooding much of New Orleans East, most of Saint Bernard Parish, and the East Bank of Plaquemines Parish. The major breaches in the city canals included one breach in the 17th St Canal, two in the London Avenue Canal, and three in the wide, navigable Industrial Canal. Flooding from the breaches put 80 percent of the city underwater for days—in many places, for weeks.

The USACE would finally admit that faulty design specifications and substandard construction of certain levee segments— not Katrina—were the primary cause of flooding in the New Orleans area.

Photo: KO

Escaping Hurricane Rita with a car full of cats and supplies. These two bonded kitties were rescued separately, but had just spent three weeks together in a 3' x 3' cage.

Chapter 30

The Dreaded
Four-Letter Word: Rita

Life changes quickly, especially on the Gulf. Just three weeks after Katrina, Hurricane Rita hit. She was dark, angry, and dangerous. As we raced out of town that Friday, September 24, Mayor Ray Nagin's announcement squealed over our car radio: "It's too late to evacuate. Do not evacuate! Stay where you are."

But there was no staying where we were. We were driving across the middle of the Route 11 Causeway Bridge, heading out of New Orleans, no other vehicles in sight. The bridge was a low-lying cement structure built so close over the water you could fish off it. But right now the bridge and water were one. Thick waves zestfully reached over the bridge and grabbed for us, toyed with us. If one wave missed, another zeroed in from the other side, like some mischievous game. We would barely make it over the bridge.

At the last minute, rescuer Nancy Cleveland and I grabbed seven cats from the MuttShack rescue outpost on Lake Pontchartrain and raced out of town. We would have left sooner, but I had a medical emergency. That morning I was out rescuing with Saskia Achilles, a slim, fast-talking Dutch girl with a heavy accent. We stumbled across a hidden condo community that everyone had missed. This boarded-up complex tucked behind a desolate neighborhood was surely full of dying animals. Knowing we had to evacuate, and yet knowing any pets would be dead when we returned, we stayed.

Rita had closed in tight as we broke into every apartment and then loaded the truck with a dozen cats and dogs. I'd just ripped off my thick leather gloves when I noticed it: We'd missed one apartment. I grabbed my crowbar and jumped out, smashing the condo window. The plate glass shattered, but with my glove removed, glass sliced deeply into my thumb. The cut was bad. Hemorrhaging. But there was nowhere to go for medical help.

With mandatory evacuation in place, the city was empty. The military had gone. Police, firemen, sheriffs, and SWAT teams already evacuated. Hospitals in greater New Orleans were still inoperable from Katrina's wrath, and the military vessel the *Iwo Jima*, with its high-tech emergency room, had pulled out of port. New Orleans was a ghost town.

Driving through the city, we came across *one* moving vehicle. *One* moving vehicle in an entire city. A new white SUV: the Army Corps of Engineers. With a first aid kit in their car, they wrapped my thumb tightly to stop the bleeding before they moved on to deal with the "other" leaks, the levees. I told them I would have my hand looked at when I got out of town but the head engineer shook his head no. "Don't wait. You need help now."

Down by the docks, in the deserted military base, we found one doctor. Charity Hospital had left a doctor and some nurses behind for any last-minute emergency. And I was it.

Rita would become one of the worst things that ever happened to animal rescue efforts. Pets fighting to survive after weeks of being isolated, with no food and water, were on their deathbeds.

But before Rita, there was hope. For the first time since Katrina, Mayor Nagin had invited residents back into the city. People began to trickle in as part of Nagin's plan to repopulate New Orleans—a plan that officials, including President George W. Bush, had questioned.

"The mayor," said Bush, "he's got this dream about having a city up and running, and we share that dream. But we also want to be realistic about some of the hurdles and obstacles that we all confront in repopulating New Orleans."

City government handed returning residents a flyer announcing a six p.m. to eight a.m. curfew and explaining that the residents may not leave their designated ZIP codes, and that numerous city services did not exist.

Welcome home, said the flyer. *You are entering at your own risk. The city of New Orleans remains a hazardous site and ongoing health and safety issues are being assessed.*

The Garden District, the Uptown neighborhood, Algiers, and the historic French Quarter had been set to reopen, bringing back one third of New Orleans' half-million inhabitants. For animals, this was a lifeline. For animal rescuers, half a million residents meant an army of volunteers marching in. And best of all, they knew where the animals were—for *they* were the owners.

But hope soon diminished when Rita, heading for Texas and Louisiana, became a hurricane to be reckoned with. Meanwhile, Dan Hitchings of the USACE warned that after Katrina the 350 miles of levees and flood walls that normally protected New Orleans were now capable of withstanding no more than "normal tidal surges."

Nagin could not ignore the threat of incoming Rita. On Monday, September 19, he ordered that the mandatory evacuation and all incoming traffic be stopped.

As we've seen, Rita was murderous, one of the worst things that ever happened to animal rescue efforts. Thousands of animals that would have lived, would have been saved just in time, perished.

As for me, I have a scar that weaves around my left thumb. The only reminder I have, not of Rita, but of the pets we saved that stormy afternoon in that hidden condo complex. Pets doomed to die there.

Yes, life changes quickly. Especially on the Gulf.

Photo: Dana Kay Deutsch. In memory of Ralphie

"Until one has loved an animal,
a part of one's soul
remains unawakened." —Anatole France

Chapter 31

Ralphie to the Rescue

Our story begins with Ralphie. Found alone, covered in tar, with a broken chain dangling from his neck, Ralphie was saved by a Katrina survivor from a flooded New Orleans junkyard. Shaved and taken to Gulfport, Mississippi, Ralphie was left in the care of rescuers.

Photo: Ralphie Series by Dana Kay Deutsch

Scared and confused, Ralphie couldn't stop shaking when he was put inside a rescuer's truck.

You wouldn't think anything could live thru this ...

... but Ralphie found a beagle.

Ralphie takes the little girl under his wing.

The next day the little girl's buddies are found.

Wait a minute—a cat? Who invited you?

Sure, it's crowded in here, but man, it's tough outside.

Ralphie sleeps while others look up and notice *another* cat has been added to the mix. These exhausted survivors became an instant family, all sharing the same destiny—and the backseat.

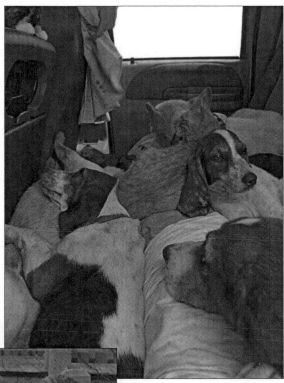

At his forever home today, Ralphie still watches out for his pals—especially his very best friend and rescuer, Dana Kay Deutsch. And the kitties? As usual, they're upstairs sunning in the window, watching their buddies below.

Chapter 32

Friends in Need

Animals were ripped from all human companionship. Strangers from all breeds and species teamed up and formed new friendships on the lonely Gulf.

Photo: KO

Photo: Michael Rieger/FEMA

Photo: Nancy Cleveland

Photo: Andrea Booher/FEMA

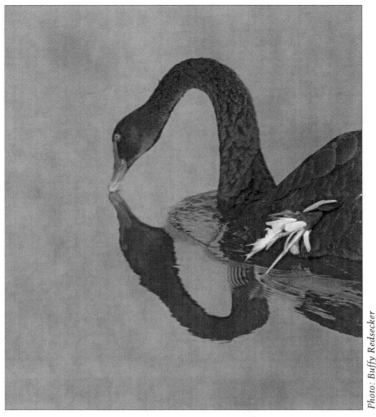

A swan with a broken wing glides through a toxic irrigation canal.

Photo: Buffy Redsecker

Chapter 33

Happily Ever After

They first met while lounging poolside in a tropical paradise. He gazed across the crystalline water and studied the lovely female swan standing poised across the pool. She glanced at him coyly, then daintily entered the water with nary a splash. Intrigued by her great beauty, he stepped into the glistening pool and swam to her side. They were made for each other. It was true love.

Okay, none of that happened. But theirs is such a beautiful love story that it should have started that way. Instead, they met in the putrid green waters of an algae-ripe pool at a destroyed grade school in northeast New Orleans.

Theirs is a love story that blossomed out of the hell and high waters of Katrina. Two black swans, both lost, each with a broken wing, would meet and fall in love. One was found floating, barely alive, down a muddy, debris-strewn irrigation canal in the middle of the suburbs; the other was found days later, miles away, dying on the side of the road near the exit ramp of an empty highway.

Both were brought to the MuttShack rescue outpost at the Lake Castle grade school off Lake Pontchartrain. With nowhere to put them, we locked them together in the fenced-off pool area behind the makeshift vet clinic.

It was love at first sight. A male with a broken right wing, a female with a broken left wing—together they made one perfect swan.

Shipped to a beautiful lake sanctuary in North Carolina, they remained inseparable. Inseparable today, tomorrow, and happily ever after.

Katrina took a toll physically and mentally on the Gulf's pets. Once playful and loving, many became dangerously aggressive.

Photo: KO

Chapter 34

Dog, Interrupted

"Roxanne was left-handed," her owner explained, smiling as he fondly remembered his chow. "She would run to you wagging her tail, then sit and lift her left paw up high. She'd always shake with her left paw. She was special," he said. "Never growled. Once she came to me with a newborn kitten in her mouth. She placed the little guy down and lay beside him. Never hurt him."

Roxanne's owners, neighbors, and vets all agree: She was a sweet, gentle, affectionate dog. Yet two weeks after Katrina she was so violent, so unmanageable, that vets at a rescue center decided there was only one way to handle her. Roxanne was killed.

Katrina left every creature in her path traumatized and distressed. Pets, normally docile and gentle, suddenly had to survive insurmountable odds in a world they no longer recognized. All were bombarded with sights, sounds, and smells they could not interpret.

A pet that had been home with loving owners was ripped from everything familiar. They were abandoned, confused, traumatized. In cases where they were rescued, they were confined in a small wire cage and surrounded by strangers. Others, not yet found by rescuers, had no food, water, or human contact. Whether bound inside their homes or running lost through the streets, these house pets were incapable of surviving, especially in this noxious, flooded land.

Animals went into survival mode. Fight or flight. For many, the primal instinct was to fight. Fight hard. Fight back. And they did. Cats and dogs often fought us with all their might. For Roxanne, it was a fight she would not win.

Perhaps you've already met Roxanne. Her owner, Robert, was forced to evacuate, leaving his two dogs, Roxanne and Angel, and his pig, Midnight [See Pet Profile: Midnight], under the I-10 Freeway in New Orleans. The three pets were then transported to the HSUS rescue center in Gonzales, Louisiana, fifty miles north of the city. Angel and Midnight would one day be returned to Robert. But Roxanne reacted violently to her rescue. Scared, stressed, locked in a cage, fighting for her life, she became fiercely aggressive, attacking all around her.

For rescuers and other Gulf volunteers, it was an all too familiar story. So often the gentle pets suffering the stress of Katrina reacted with aggression. So often they were "euthanized" in the overcrowded system lacking the time, funding, or manpower to help them. With thousands of animals being rescued and pushed into shelters, there was little time to evaluate what was real aggression and what was nothing more than fear-induced aggression—a temporary reaction to change and chaos.

For a long time no one had the heart to tell Robert what really happened to Roxanne. But now he knows. After a month of anger, pain, and sorrow, he told me it still hurts him to think of how her life ended. But he had to let her go. Let her go from his heart to a better place. And every morning, he stops by the underpass of the I-10 where he left her and says a prayer for her. "Not sometimes, not once, not occasionally," he reminds me, "but every single day I stop there and say a prayer for her."

May sweet Roxanne, misunderstood in the most traumatic days of her life, rest in peace. May she rest in peace with all her kindred spirits who died the same way, believing that in order to survive they would have to put up the fight of their lives.

We Can Make a Difference

It should be made illegal to terminate pets rescued from catastrophes unless there are serious health issues and they need to be euthanized, meaning "put out of their misery in a true mercy killing." That's the real meaning of euthanize; it is not the endless killing of healthy animals that goes on all day—every day—in America's "shelters." Euthanasia is only for seriously ill or injured animals, to "put them out of their misery." To use the word randomly, as we do in the USA when describing animals killed in our shelters, is a grave injustice.

Pets found in emergencies that are cage-aggressive, animal-aggressive, and became violent due to stress, must be given the space and time to adjust. On the Gulf, all temporary shelters were overcrowded, with few caretakers, behaviorists, or vets available, leaving few options. Plans must be made so this never happens again. Donation funds could be allocated for behaviorists to work with traumatized, confused animals.

Part 2

AS THE DUST SETTLED

After leaving the Gulf for two weeks in late November to film a documentary on orphans in Cambodia, I returned to New Orleans to help our own orphans of the storm. On this trip I relocated to St. Bernard Parish, the hard-hit parish, or county, below the Ninth Ward, next to New Orleans.

The situation in the Gulf was forever changing. Animals were more and more resistant to our help. Rescuers had come and gone, and residents were filtering back home hoping to find their pets alive and to salvage any personal possessions.

Chapter 35

Running on Empty

A s night crept into downtown New Orleans, the dog appeared out of nowhere. He came bounding around the debris-strewn corner so quickly I thought he was being chased. But he was alone. A German shepherd: emaciated, confused. Even though I had dog food in my hand, he sped off the second he saw me. To this confused dog, I was the enemy.

In the early days after Katrina, lost pets would scramble to rescuers, looking for food and reassurance, seeking the human companionship they knew so well and missed so much. But weeks later, life on the streets took its toll and all the rules had changed. Wandering alone, traumatized pets viewed everything as a threat and people were just one more danger to avoid. For these pets, the bond with mankind was no more. For them, the human touch and voice were foreign. We called them runners. Runners: one small, deadly word.

With so many animals needing help all around and so few people to save them, we had little time for the futile chase after runners. Yet they were everywhere. Cats, dogs—the streets were full of these fast, terrified souls. We'd all attempt to catch them; everyone wanted to help the runners, but it was hopeless. We pursued them on foot, in cars, up streets, around buildings. We tried to trap them, corral them, corner them. But the results were always the same; they would scurry under the maze of buildings and vanish from sight. For pets, we were the enemy. For us, precious time was lost—time needed to save other animals in jeopardy.

Runners were the saddest lot of all, the anguish of animal rescuers. In this grim city with little food and water, the more they ran, the more energy they wasted, and the quicker they died.

I'd try to convince myself that at least they died their way-running. Running free. But the truth was that they were just running. Running scared.

Chapter 36

Conversation with a Cat

"Chris, be careful when you open the car door. She's in here, somewhere," I said.

"Or so you say," he replied.

Photographer Chris Gubbels wasn't my only passenger that night driving around the Ninth Ward. For days I had a kitty living in my rental car. A kitty Chris had never seen. She was burrowed under the backseat, hidden tight, scared to death. My car was her carrier, her personal SUV cat carrier on wheels.

This was one of those times when there was "no room at the inn," when temporary shelters around the Gulf were full.

"We're not taking pets," intake groups up north told us. "No room, we're backed up." This was a problem for all rescuers; you'd have a car full of animals and nowhere to send them. Rescuing was often a game of musical chairs and this time the music had stopped and I was left standing, with no chair and four cats.

I lived on a ship at this time. Like most volunteers, we moved from area to area, wherever we were needed. This was my fourth "home" on the Gulf. When I arrived in New Orleans, I started out in the Winn-Dixie parking lot. Then I moved to the grounds of a destroyed grade school, Lake Castle, on Lake Pontchartrain to help at MuttShack. Next, I moved to assist the pets of St. Bernard Parish, the district beneath the Ninth Ward. I lived on a cruise ship there for a few days—the *Scotia Prince*, brought in from Canada as a temporary residence for St. Bernard Parish employees, including firemen, police, and relief workers. My rescued kitten, King Kong, and I got thrown off the ship when they found her stowed away in my room. Homeless again, I was generously given a room aboard the *Belatrix*, a thousand-foot-long merchant marine ship made of acres of cold gray steel.

With permission, I moved three cats into my room on the *Belatrix*: a tall tabby with a pin in her back leg, a black feral, and my recently rescued gray kitty, the tiny but aptly named King Kong.

With a room full of cats on board, I kept this new black and white kitty in my van. She was the "shy" type—okay, "invisible." I'd leave a litter box and food out when I parked the van for the night. The food was gone and the litter box used by morning, but the kitty was never seen.

Chris, a photographer from Missouri, didn't talk much but you'd hear him all day by the whirl of his camera. He hitched a ride down in a Best Friends Animal Society delivery truck from their temporary rescue center in Mississippi. They were bringing me sixty thousand pounds of Kibbles and Bits. That sounds like a lot of food, but it would last a few hours, distributed to drop points for the strays of St. Bernard Parish. I had made a deal with the military to deliver this food to drop-off points around the city. Best Friends, and others, were donating food that had been donated to them. I was then donating it to other rescue groups and they would donate it to the strays. Everything was a multi-leveled hand-me-down. Happily, I inherited Chris, who wanted to stay and photograph the city.

That night we were driving around the Lower Ninth Ward. The Ninth, shown as a pile of splinters in press photos, ran along the river where the Industrial Canal overtopped. The Ninth received much of the publicity when the city flooded, but many areas of the city and the Gulf were just as devastated.

Bored as we drove through the dark, desolate streets, I let out a "meow," a pretty good imitation of a cat. After a moment, Chris responded with a soft meow. I eyed him, impressed by his ability to speak feline.

"Not bad," I said. "In cat speak, I give that an eight on a scale of ten."

"That wasn't me," Chris said.

I turned to the back of the SUV, where the unseen cat was buried somewhere under the backseat and rescue debris.

"That was *her?*"

"Wasn't me," he said.

Thus began one of the most fascinating discussions I have ever had. An hour-long, in-depth conversation with a cat. I have no idea what we discussed, but apparently it was very important, and for once I said all the right things, as I convinced a shy, scared kitty that I was her buddy. Her very own BFF (Best Feline Friend).

I would meow and she would respond. I spoke, she answered. She spoke, I answered. Again and again our repartee continued. Her meows were clear and distinct—some were long and questioning, some short and brusque. There were soft meows, crackling meows, angry meows, and two-part meows. She had an extensive vocabulary. She would speak up and wait for me to answer each time. And if I answered the wrong way, she replied with an exasperated meow. "Pay attention," she complained.

These meows were not random sounds. She was speaking to me with what seemed to be an emotional and well-formed vocabulary. Dozens of words. Having spent a lifetime on the road learning languages, I have an ear for the subtleties of spoken sounds. I listened in awe as she spoke. If I didn't answer her, she would repeat herself again and again, the same sound, as if trying to make a point. I would scramble to figure out what the right response was. Should I utter a quick meow? A two-part meow? A long, singsong meow? She spoke a detailed, expressive language all its own—yet the cat remained unseen.

Her meows grew louder as she inched closer, under the seats, approaching from the rear of the car. Suddenly, I felt a tap on my shoulder. I turned quickly to see her, now face-to-face. She was standing up, her two feet on the backseat, stretching up, resting her front feet on the back of my chair. With one paw, she tapped my shoulder again.

By the end of the night, we had come to an agreement. I guess I told her she was free to roam the van, then I must have asked her to stretch across the dashboard and go to sleep, since that's what she did next.

New Orleans was an uncharted land where rescuer and animal became one; we were in it together, alone in a brutal, deadly world. And we had our own ways of communicating; a need to express; a desire to be understood.

Days later when Chris left town he took this cat home and fostered her. She now lives somewhere in Missouri and no longer has in-depth conversations with anyone. I guess in that dark, quiet night in New Orleans she'd said all she had to say—for a lifetime.

We Can Make a Difference

Shelters and foster homes are overcrowded due to the out-of-control breeding of pets. The old paradigm was that one unaltered cat and her offspring will cause the birth of over 400,000 cats in just seven years. (If she has one litter of seven, and those seven have seven, and each of those seven cats have seven, etc., the myth is that one fertile cat could exponentially cause the birth of over 400,000 cats.)

These numbers have proven to be unrealistic. The University of Washington found that one unaltered cat and her seven kittens would create about 200 offspring in seven years. That is still 200 too many. The damage caused by one fertile animal becomes a death sentence for many pets already in our overflowing system. In the case of America's pets BIRTH = DEATH. Many pets already here do not have homes; we should not create more litters. Remember, if you want to save lives and help stop the slaughter of innocent animals, please spay and neuter. It really is that simple.

(Some say there are enough homes, but the pounds are not trying hard enough to place animals. True or not, it doesn't matter—having fewer animals would still lighten the load, and the killing would ease up.)

If only we could get politicians to wake up and smell the decomposing pets strewn across our national dump sites. They used our tax money to bail out banks, auto companies, and Wall Street con artists—why not spend money protecting America's innocent animals? I don't expect altruism in Washington, but how about using spay/neuter as a money-saving, job-creating industry?

Get the pets out of the killing factories we call shelters and offer subsidies vets and vet techs to spay/neuter nationwide. If any politician wants to join me, contact me. I invite you to tour the overcrowded, expensive-to-maintain shelters to see what life there is *really* like. It costs a lot less to have government-sponsored spay/neuter programs across the USA than to pay for the intake, housing, death, and disposal of the millions of animals killed yearly in our shelters.

(Death in a shelter can mean the pet is stuffed into an outdated gas chamber and suffocated by noxious fumes, or the brutal heart stick is slammed into their chest.)

Let's go, Washington. Do the math. All this needless killing is a disgrace to our country.

Chapter 37

Allen's Story

The dog was fast, clever, wary ... and somebody's boy. Somebody's lost, terrorized boy.

I found him downtown near the projects on the mean streets of a place known as Fort Apache. The dog lived under the massive cement underbelly of the I-10 freeway. Beneath this concrete monster was a wide center divider that locals called neutral ground. Like all neutral ground in New Orleans, this was now a resting place for hundreds of wrecked cars that floodwaters had hustled into the streets and that tow trucks had plucked back out. There he was, curled up tight, fending off that cold, windy day: a scarred, matted dog alone on this island, traffic swirling all around.

He was a mix—part chow, part Lab, part who knows what. He wore a collar with an ID tag, but it was impossible to get that close. I named him "Allen" after the street sign nearby. And as I would soon find out, his whole life had changed right there on the corner, on the corner of North Claiborne and Allen Street.

I loved that dog right away. Something about him, those innocent eyes, his soft demeanor. I remember thinking he should be sleeping on a shaded porch or playing in a grassy backyard. Sweet, shy, gentle—he didn't belong to the streets.

For days I stopped by and called him, summoned him out of the junked cars. He'd peek out from behind a rusty bumper and listen, then come closer, closer. He'd come so close I could almost touch him. He was trying hard to connect but then he'd run. Run far enough to be safe. Far enough to keep an eye on me. Far enough to vanish into the maze of battered autos.

A skinny black man with a limp hustled up to me as Allen and I went through the daily routine. "You never gonna catch him," the man warned. "Been here months, since Katrina. Never seen him 'fore that. He'll come close, but you never gonna get him."

The man was right.

Allen was impossible to catch; a rescuer's nightmare. Living at a dangerous intersection, we feared he would get hit. For days we tried everything short of drugging him. Drugging him was too dangerous at this intersection. Besides, it was a last resort.

At night we left safe metal traps piled high inside with ripe steak, bacon, dog food—whatever scraps we could dig up in this shell of a city. Sometimes I'd watch him from across the street as he would enter the trap, one foot … two … then change his mind, exit. No matter how hungry he was, he was not going to leave that corner. He was not going to lose his freedom. Yeah, I loved that dog right away.

But Allen wasn't our only concern. Lost pets were starving all over the city. Feeding stations had to be refilled, pets rescued, traps checked. Nancy Cleveland and I stopped by for days to check on Allen. Nancy, a first-time rescuer from Chicago, turned up on the Gulf just like I did, and we went *way* back. In New Orleans, that meant back to the floods. Nancy was always serious, introspective, but then she'd glow with a floodlight smile, just to keep you guessing.

On day two of the Allen saga, I borrowed a camera. If I could get the dog close enough, I could zoom in on his tag. I kept clicking away, but the tag had to hang just right to read it. Finally, a good shot. Nancy blew it up on the computer and there it was—a phone number. A connection to his past.

Calling the number on the tag, we reached a pet registry. We got the owner's phone number, his address, and Allen's real name. His name was Duchess. Allen was a girl.

I jumped out of the rescue car and called to her. "Duchess, Duchess." But the dog wandered off, uninterested. Her name seemed just a foggy memory from another life; it meant nothing anymore.

We dialed the owner's number as we dashed to the address. Duchess lived six miles away in the suburb of Gentilly. But the news wasn't good. Like most numbers in New Orleans, this phone was disconnected with no forwarding. The house was vacated, rubble. We left a note on the porch with our phone number. All we could do now was wait.

Days later, her owner, McNeal Cayette, drove in from Houston to search for Duchess and check on his house. Finding our note, he called instantly, then raced to the junkyard beneath the I-10, ecstatic to see his beloved pet. But the dog was gone. McNeal canvassed the area and returned for days, but would never find his Duchess again. He still searches that district for her, but she has never been seen.

"Duchess was a sweet girl," he remembers. "Daddy's little girl. She was never on her own. Never. Except for our daily walks together, she was always in the house with me, or safe in the backyard." For the last two years, Duchess was his only family.

After the floods, McNeal waded through waist-high water with Duchess paddling at his side as he strained to keep her from drowning. Leaving her on neutral ground, he was escorted to the helicopter waiting on the freeway overhead. He cried as he untied her leash and was forced to evacuate. Forced to leave her behind.

And there we found her, months later, exactly where she'd been left. Right there, near the projects, on the mean streets of a place known as Fort Apache. Under the massive cement underbelly of the I-10 freeway. Right there on the corner, the corner of North Claiborne and Allen Street.

UPDATE: Almost a year after McNeal Cayette had to leave Allen behind in New Orleans, he contacted me. Here is our correspondence:

Karen,

I don't know if you remember me, but I am the owner of Auggie Doggie (or Duchess), a dog you attempted to rescue in New Orleans who would not be captured. Well, I have good news. Auggie Doggie has been found. While visiting New Orleans on the weekend of July 30th {2006} Auggie was found less than ten blocks from where I left her more than eleven months earlier. She was still wearing the same red collar (minus the tag), and seemed to still have been living in the streets, but in excellent health. I have since carried her back to Houston, had her checked out by a vet, and she has received a clean bill of health. Thank you so much for your leads which aided to my eventually finding her. She is currently enjoying being back with me and trying to adjust to apartment living (just like me). I am including a picture.

Cayette,

Wow! I am so happy for you. True, if we never spotted Allen (Duchess) you may have never found her. I am so glad we could help after all! CONGRATULATIONS. (How did she react? Did you call her name and she came to you? Or did she run?)

_____

Karen,

Duchess was spotted by one of the neighborhood people I had left contact information with. It just happened to be a weekend when my girlfriend and I were in town. (We both had known Duchess since a puppy.) My girlfriend went and picked her up and she immediately responded to her voice and her name and came running. She then called me to tell me she had found Duchess, and she put the phone to her ears. When she heard my voice she started licking the telephone. When I finally saw her later she first did a second take and then came running. She is adjusting to apartment living but we walked all day long. Thanks again for everything.

Cayette

Photo: McNeal Cayette

"If you are not too long, I will wait here for all my life."
—Oscar Wilde

Chapter 38

There's No Place Like Home

In downtown New Orleans this little girl was tied to the fire hydrant by her owner, who then jumped on a bus and vanished. Hours later she was still waiting patiently. Waiting to go home. But she'd been abandoned there; her owner never returned. She watched curiously as every car passed and she stood to greet the occasional resident who ambled by. But no one stopped for her.

Long after Katrina, many pets that survived the hurricane and floods were reunited with owners who themselves had nowhere to live. New Orleans was fast becoming a city full of abandoned and surrendered animals. With local foster homes and rescues overcrowded and few residents returning to the city, pets would now receive the final blow. Their last days would be spent locked in narrow metal cages at county shelters until their time was up.

This little girl was one of the few lucky ones. She now lives in New York and will never be abandoned again.

Photo: KO

You can see the varying water lines on this statue, from her chin down to her knees, yet she was never knocked over in the flood. These defiant statues were everywhere.

Chapter 39

The Myth of the Virgin Mary

New Orleans had been a city bubbling with music, culture, history, and religion. Rescuers couldn't help but notice how many front lawns throughout residential neighborhoods displayed Virgin Mary statues. We were always amazed that these statues pulled through the storm unscathed, no matter how much destruction surrounded them. It was an odd phenomenon.

The indestructibility of the Virgin Mary statuary was a myth circulating throughout New Orleans.

Photo: Chris Gubbels

Chapter 40

Happy Birthday

I never cried in New Orleans. No matter what I saw, no matter what death and destruction I walked through, there was no time for tears, no time for self. An internal filter had taken over, a shield that numbed me from the pain, protected me from the sights. You couldn't allow yourself to feel. Once you started feeling in New Orleans, you were through—of no use to rescuers, residents, or the pets of the city. But for me, all that changed with two words: Chance and Justice.

It was my birthday, November 11, 2005. I was supposed to have left New Orleans by then to resume my life. But New Orleans had a tight grip on all of us. I had an event to attend

153

at the Beverly Hills Hotel, a toast for screenwriters, for Nicholl Fellows. The Academy of Motion Picture Arts and Sciences, the "Oscar" people, were throwing a formal dinner for us. Normally, I'd be thrilled to be a guest, honored among other Nicholl Fellows at our annual award ceremony, but this year I was honored to be right where I was.

On the morning of my birthday I headed down a bayou road in St. Bernard Parish, a district below the Ninth Ward. The road ran along a steely gray bayou; the swampy waters fidgeted with alligators and turtles.

After miles, the road ended. A river interrupted, halting the street mid-sentence. To my right, there was an open steel gate holding back a dirt road. A string of a road that unraveled into the forest then curved out of sight.

I followed the road into the woods and came upon a clearing: a perfectly coiffed pasture, a haven of calm among these dark, ghostly woods. New white fences framed acres of cut grass, now burnt from the toxic flood. There were two horse barns in front of me and a bigger barn off to the right. These matching stables of glossy white wood with crisp green trim were quaint, picturesque. This was a fairy-tale horse farm.

I stood for a moment as I gazed at the silent buildings. What if the horses were still here? What if they ...? No. These were prize horses. This seemed to be a farm for purebreds. Surely they had been evacuated.

I stepped closer and saw the first horse. He was hanging from a tree, his neck broken, his limp body dragging in the dirty bayou water. I paused as my heart banged around in my chest as if readjusting itself. Once it settled, I continued on. Again, my filter saved me. I had seen a few thousand dead animals by then, seen other stables, other drowned horses. My filter was working perfectly. My screen was up and it was locked tight. It was business as usual. I could move forward.

I entered the first barn; it was jammed against the bank of the overflowing bayou. The wooden doors of the stalls inside were shut, locked tight by heavy steel bars. I peeked into the first stall … and the second. These tightly-sealed tombs each contained a dead white horse, sprawled out, decomposing in the mud.

I could tell by the water level near the ceiling and the kick marks halfway up the walls that these horses swam and struggled before they died. The top waterline, where the bayou first settled, was two feet below the ceiling. I realized that when the water barged in, the horses were lifted up and swam in their stalls. They had a two-foot air pocket. Their swift feet kicked, hitting the walls halfway up, as they fought to keep their heads above water.

Horses are excellent swimmers. I was sure these two swam for a long time before they grew too weak and drowned. I had no feelings about it. My protective filters were in full gear. And even though I knew that somewhere deep inside I was hemorrhaging from these images, I was protected from them and could remain logical, steadfast, and most importantly, unemotional. No time to waste with the dead; in New Orleans there was only time for the living.

As I stepped away from the two horses, I noticed words engraved on their stalls. Name plaques with letters neatly inscribed into the steel trim on their doors.

Photo: KO

One horse was Chance, the other Justice.

Chance and Justice. These were their names. I didn't want to know their names. I didn't want to get that personal. But it was too late. They were no longer rotting corpses; I knew their names. They had a human family who loved them. Who raised them, cherished them—and named them. A family who would find them here, like this, and forever be scarred. Eternally wounded. And suddenly it hit me. All of it—the torturous days, the heart-wrenching weeks. My filter burst like the levees themselves and my emotions flooded, wreaking havoc. Every feeling that I had suppressed, ignored, denied, now slapped me in the face, all screaming for attention. How dare I shut them out? The images surrounded me. The dead, the dying—everywhere. Humans, cats, dogs, parrots, raccoons, birds, deer—every one of them shouting, demanding to be heard, begging to be recognized, wanting to be remembered. And here were these two palominos, Tennessee Walking Horses named Chance and Justice.

Just weeks ago these elite athletes pranced in this grassy field outside. They were proud. They were safe. They were free. They were loved. Their shiny, brushed manes reflected the warm summer light. Their painted black hooves kicked dirt as their muscular legs dug in. And no doubt bunnies, soft and jumpy, watched them nervously from distant grass, and birds flitted past to feed their plump fledglings nearby. The horses, the birds, the bunnies. All gone. All gone. All gone. I walked off to find the horses' barn mates. There were sixteen more. All had names. All had died tragic deaths, without a chance, without justice. I never cried in New Orleans, but this time I sobbed.

A Survivor Speaks...

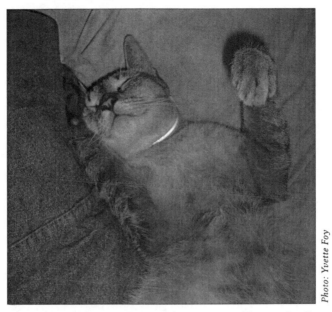

Photo: Yvette Foy

After months of struggling on the streets, Mikko can finally sleep peacefully in the backseat.

Chapter 41

Finding Mikko

By Yvette Foy

Dear Friends, Strangers, and Caring Pet Community,

After nine months, three weeks, and two days I am wonderfully happy to announce that we found our cat, Mikko.

On Friday, June 23, 2006, we drove from Houston, TX, to Atlanta, GA, stopping in New Orleans for the night. On more than five occasions I had been back to our home in the Gentilly area of New Orleans to salvage memorabilia and look for our missing cat, Mikko. We had two cats prior to Hurricane Katrina.

On my first visit back to the city in October 2005, one of our cats, Gus, came running to the front lawn when I called his name. He was scared and jittery but he recognized my voice and came running for rescue. I called and called for Mikko, but he did not come. I went back several times that visit and even left an item of clothing as suggested, but he did not return at my bidding.

I visited in November, December, and finally in January—no Mikko. Many champions for pets surfaced throughout that time, tirelessly searching any lead that would help us find our missing cat.

I never gave up hope and never allowed my daughter to give up hope. I told her that he had probably been caught by rescuers and adopted by a nice family somewhere across the country. I refused to give away his cloth cat carrier, salvaged from the garage ruins. It sat on our back porch, waiting.

As we drove into the outskirts of New Orleans on the way to Georgia, nostalgia rose like the tide at sunset. I had the strongest urge to visit our home—now gutted and overrun with grass. I drove to the exit and approached stealthily; it was 10:30 p.m.

The main thoroughfare of Elysian Fields, once bustling, was now quiet and bleak. My daughter and I circled the block slowly as we talked about the neighborhood. Dim lights peered out from FEMA trailers on the neighboring streets. The Baptist church on the opposite corner had been razed, its bare frame blackened by fire and smoke. In stark contrast to the refurbished dwellings nearby, and the vacant homes still marked with scarlet-colored spray paint, all decorated the scene before us. As we spoke in hushed tones and surveyed the new beginnings, my eyes darted to a small figure, frozen in anticipation, on the neighboring lawn as our vehicle approached. I halted my daughter in mid-sentence with one ghastly phrase: "That's Mikko!"

I stopped the car and rolled the window down. I began calling his name. The queerest look came over his face. I'll never forget it. It was as if he was searching through his memory for a time when he didn't have to scrounge through a deserted, hurricane-ravaged neighborhood for food and water; fend off predators, disease, and harsh elements; and back to when a lady and a girl loved him, gave him a home, and called him Mikko. He began to meow.

My daughter, Epiphany, jumped out of the car and walked to him. He was skittish and untrusting but she kept calling his name. He threw himself onto the ground and began squirming the way he would when he wanted someone to pet and scratch him. I sat in the car in total shock. It took us a while, but we got him into the car and calmed him down.

We drove Mikko back to Houston. He is adjusting well. He has been pretty jumpy, but I remember Gus reacted the same way when I rescued him after the storm. Oh yeah, Gus. I think Gus had gotten adjusted to our house being a one-cat home again. We adopted Gus one year before Mikko. He had always viewed Mikko as a disgusting little brother who followed him around and mimicked his every move.

Mikko has staked new territory on a rug underneath my bed. He has also taken to prancing around the rooftops of houses in Houston—a feat that makes my daughter quite nervous, but one I'm sure he acquired during his tenure in post-hurricane New Orleans.

Those of you reading this may or may not understand exactly what happened to the pet owners prior to Katrina. Many of them were not able to transport or evacuate their pets. I was one such pet owner. I am an event manager. I had traveled to Miami on business the Wednesday before the storm. Neither my daughter nor I were in New Orleans and our cats had been entrusted to my father and my friend. I was only to be gone away on business one week. Hurricane Katrina hit the coast of Florida on Thursday afternoon while I was in Miami. It was accompanied by strong winds and rain. On Friday, as I sat at my computer and perused the Weather Channel, I saw that Hurricane Katrina had re-entered the Gulf of Mexico on a northwestward path.

I remember thinking nonchalantly, "That doesn't look good." I closed my computer to head out the door for a busy weekend of preparing for award show parties. I heard of the residential panic in New Orleans through a casual call to a friend to rave about the celebrity presence in Miami. The news sent me into a tailspin. I began calling family and friends to gather information on their evacuation plan. Everyone was busy preparing to leave. No one could take my cats.

I am grateful that my brother evacuated my father. I am grateful that at my request he pulled open the staircase to the attic in my house. He also gathered my photos, memorabilia, and computer hard drive and transported them in a plastic bag out of the city that would soon be submerged.

I am most grateful for my friend, Wendy, who stopped at my house to place all my cat food and a huge pot of fresh water in the attic. She led the cats to the stairs, thereby laying out the hurricane escape route. The veterinarian would later quote, "That probably saved their lives." She and her family took initial refuge in the Federal Reserve Bank, where her husband is employed.

I am grateful for each person who went to my house and called out my cats' names in an effort to rescue them for me. I am grateful for my neighbors, whoever they are, wherever they are, who continue to feed stray cats and dogs separated from their loved ones by this horrific tragedy.

And I am most grateful for you who are reading this—you who may have sent my missing cat messages to everyone on your e-mail list; you who forwarded pictures, initiated rescue efforts, searched Pet Finders listings and reports, reunited families and pets, fostered pets, facilitated adoptions; and you who prayed for the safe return, rescue, or care of the animals affected by the disaster in the Gulf Coast region.

May God bless you and keep you.

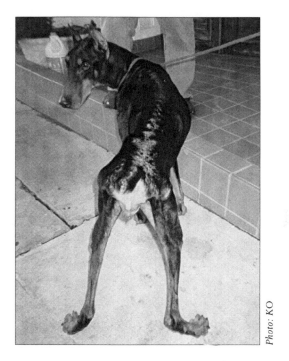

Chapter 42

At Long Last, Love

I t was late October of 2005 when I saw the Doberman, Leibchen, struggling to stand outside a vet's office in New Orleans.
"Is she the one they threw out in the trash?" I asked the girl
beside her.

"Yeah."

"That's two dogs I know of. Same thing with a cocker spaniel."

While some Gulf residents will search for their cherished pets
for the rest of their lives, a few families returned home afraid of
the animals they'd left behind. Afraid their now dying pets would
make them sick from the deadly toxins they'd ingested, or cost

a fortune in vet bills. Other owners, now homeless themselves, reluctantly dropped pets off at rescue centers.

For a handful of Katrina evacuees, however, pets were never much more than an inconvenience. Apparently this poor dog belonged to *that* category of owner: the uncaring, unloving pet owner.

Leibchen was barely able to lift her head when her owners returned, so they dragged her to the trash outside to be hauled off to the city dump. She was discarded like all other wet debris torn from her demolished home—a home she starved in alone for seven weeks, waiting for her owners to return.

When a concerned neighbor noticed the dog was still alive in the trash, she alerted the owners, who told her not to worry—the dog would be "dead by morning." Leibchen was rescued and taken to a foster home to live out her days. Unfortunately, like many Gulf pets, her body was severely compromised by the trauma of weeks without food and water. She lived only a few more months, but for once in her life her days were full of warmth, attention, and at long last, love.

Photo: Mary Thompson

New Orleans wasn't exempt from the nationwide disgrace of chaining, or "tethering," innocent pets. For some animals, Katrina was the best thing that ever happened to them. They were finally saved.

Chapter 43

Dirty Little Secrets

W e found it all—every category of animal abuse was recognizable among the pets we rescued. The pitiful dogs chained to fences that knew no other life; the once innocent pit bulls taught to kill; the mangled, scarred "bait" dogs thrown into the ring as practice to fight on; and the emaciated dogs racked with mange, their collars embedded so deeply into their necks they had to be surgically removed.

At times what we discovered was so horrific, it is better left unsaid. What I cannot even bare to describe, these animals *lived*. For these pets, Katrina was the best thing that ever happened to them. Though she covered the city deep in contaminated floods

163

swirling with debris, she also led us to find and save these pets that had been scarred by cruelty and abuse.

Upon discovering these pets, we questioned mankind. As a nation how could we allow this? As pet owners, how could we treat innocent beings this way? The good news: For every human who abused a pet, hundreds of rescuers and relief workers did everything to save them. For every pet neglected by its owners, hundreds of owners adored and respected their animals.

We Can Make a Difference

I hope we open our eyes to the innocent animals that suffer across our nation every day, in every city and town. I hope we take it upon ourselves to expose the dirty little secrets we see, sometimes right next door.

While animal abuse is everywhere, the laws protecting pets are lagging far behind. Murdering and torturing animals will often get abusers a small fine and misdemeanor charges.

Animals suffer in silence. We must be their voice. If you see anything suspicious, report it. And again, be careful; not only are Class B dealers and bunchers looking for animals, dog fighters also use innocent pets as bait. Baiting is the act of tormenting a confined animal by setting *dogs* upon it for sport. The dogs attack the opposing animal, biting and tearing at it to incapacitate or kill it. This is all to practice for when they are in the arena, fighting for entertainment and gambling. While dog fighting is illegal in the U.S., it is still practiced underground nationwide.

While many cities post *No skating on the sidewalks* signs, New Orleans sends out a different message.

Photo: KO

If you see an animal that is badly scarred, it's possible it is used for bait. Call the authorities. We must be the voice for animals.

Photo: Nancy Cleveland

A rescued cat will be shipped into "the system," her final fate unknown.

Chapter 44

Fighting the System

The one thing rescuers feared most is the system —that cold, hardened, deadly maze of high-kill animal shelters that stretch across America. Every time we rescued a Katrina pet we knew we were endangering the *other* animals already stuck in the system, animals that had been abandoned and surrendered nationwide. Innocent souls already needing homes across America would now be passed over, lose their only chance, when an unexpected 15,000 homeless Katrina pets now needed the space

Katrina caused a quick and deadly overload on the nation's shelters and foster homes. With great sympathy for citizens of the Gulf, people were drawn to Katrina's sorrowful pets. Americans watching the heartbreaking images from the Gulf felt hopeless and stepped up to help. Katrina pets were in high demand, coming with a built-in marketing campaign. They were hurricane survivors and had lived through one of the greatest natural disasters in our history. Often just having the word *Katrina* on their paperwork assured them a home. Meanwhile, shelter pets nationwide would now pay with their lives, and it was this displacement rescuers feared.

Were we rescuing a pet on the Gulf only to cause the death of another already ensnared in the system? And worse, there was no guarantee these Katrina pets themselves could survive the deadly system.

We Can Make a Difference

Having witnessed firsthand the disgrace of our overcrowded national "shelter" system and becoming aware of the vast number of animals senselessly killed, there has to be a change. Right now, on a very low average, an estimated six million pets are killed yearly in our shelters. That's half a million a month, about 17,000 a day, or 2,125 an hour, In the time it just took you to read the statistics in this sentence, thirty-five animals were killed somewhere in the U.S., either by injection, being stuffed into a gas chamber, or by an often brutal "heart stick."

America cannot be proud of what seems to be our motto: *Breed many, adopt a few, kill most.* We must replace this motto with four honorable words: *We spay and neuter.* Again, one of the most important things you can do to improve our horrific system is that simple: please spay and neuter.

Our language in this country must also change. Most animals are killed unnecessarily in our antiquated "shelter" system. Our tax money is allocated for animal "care and control," yet a large percentage of our money is spent for their extermination. They are neither being "sheltered" nor "cared" for. Nor are we "putting them to sleep," "putting them down," or merely "euthanizing" them— we're killing them. Millions every year. The glossy terms mask the true horror of what is going on in this country where our shelters, to be frank, are getting away with murder.

The definition of euthanize is *to mercifully end a life due to a terminal health condition.* Very few shelter animals are killed for this reason. They are killed because they are considered un-adopt-able, because their cage is needed, because they are a common color such as black, because they are seniors, because they are newborns, because they have a cough...

Today our nation is in an upheaval over the extermination of animals. A national no-kill movement is in its infancy, crawling along as rescuers and the animal loving population have seen enough of the "death and destruction" created by "care and control."

Finally, some savvy taxpayers are filing Freedom of Information Acts against counties to expose their shelter's inner workings; shelters are being held accountable and taken to court for cruelty. Today lawsuits have reared their heads as animal advocates try to shut down what is believed to be the barbaric, outdated method of using gas chambers to kill pets. For more information on the no-kill movement, read the groundbreaking book *Redemption*, by attorney Nathan Winograd.

Another way you can fight the system and help animals is to stop buying pets from stores, puppy mills, and backyard breeders. Every time you buy a pet, you've made one less home available for the animals already stuck in the system. Thus the saying, "For every pet you buy, a shelter pet will die."

If your heart is set on a purebred dog or cat—great. Thirty percent of all pets in our shelters are purebreds. Check online and through your local no-kill groups for a list of purebred rescues in your own community.

Photo: Tracy Kilpatrick

Chapter 45

The Mardi Gras Gang

Six months after Katrina, during the first post-hurricane Mardi Gras, puppies were found at this Ninth Ward address. The pups were affectionately named The Mardi Gras Gang. Rescue efforts were delayed and police alerted when animal rescuers discovered a human body in the wreckage.

A Rescuer Remembers...

Photo: Kristina Rieck

Taz was so aggressive, his crate carried
the warning: Very Feral.

Chapter 46

TAZ: King of the Ferals

By Nancy Cleveland

A gray tiger kitten bounced across Claiborne Avenue in front of me. I slammed on the brakes as it disappeared into the high grass of a corner lot, scurrying among the flooded cars and broken debris of gutted homes.

I followed the kitten's path into the grass and saw it, or maybe its sister, scramble over a crumbled concrete wall behind a bright orange house. Walking along the sidewalk I passed a robin's egg-blue home tucked among the row of multi-colored pastel houses, all with high, louvered windows and carved woodwork adorning their battered facades. The watermarks here on Spain Street were only a few feet high, unlike some parts of the city where water went over the roofs or washed away buildings completely.

169

European craftsmen constructed these houses in the 1920s, lured with promises of high pay and decent homes at the height of New Orleans' wealth and power, when it was the richest city in the south and one of the financial trading centers of the nation.

"My grandfather built this house," said returning resident Jamie, nodding towards his house. "When he wasn't building other people's homes." Jamie was back, working to repair his family's heritage. His wife and daughter, evacuated during Katrina by National Guard helicopters, were still in Texas.

"Right before the hurricane, this was a drug dealers' war zone," Jamie said. "Most dangerous place in the city. You step outside, they're shooting each other *allatime*, up an' down the street."

Now the street was virtually abandoned except for a dog pack that ran at night, three or four chows and pit bull mixes. "They come right to me, want to eat. I don't go out when I see them," Jamie said.

He told me he fed cats sometimes in his backyard with scraps from the Red Cross meals given out free across the city. In the narrow alley beside Jamie's home, I spotted two tiger kittens tumbling over their mom and a small black and white cat that stared intently at me. He emerged from under the building and I noticed his head was twisted, painfully cranked to one side, often a sign of an inner ear infection, which can destroy a cat's sense of balance.

"I call him Gimpy," Jamie said. " 'Cause he walks funny."

The little black and white Gimpy leaped at a butterfly and missed, jumping crooked instead of straight. How could he hunt to eat? He needed help, definitely. I volunteered to take Gimpy to a vet and asked Jamie if I could put a trap on his back porch. He agreed.

We took turns watching it and in two weeks I nabbed two cats. A big yellow tiger and a tabby Tom. No kittens. No Gimpy. Cat trapping was frustrating. You seldom got the cat you tried for. You'd go for obviously a beloved pet, the dainty calico female with a rhinestone collar that meowed but shied away, too scared to come close—but you'd get the bruiser tomcat with no ears and a nasty disposition who wanted to take your hand off.

I finally got Gimpy late one February afternoon. Tuna fish was the bait that lured him. Some cats deal with being in a trap very calmly. They'll even sniff your hand and rub on it, asking to be petted. Some hide in the back. Others growl or hiss to show they're not afraid. Some attack.

When I reached down to see if he was friendly, Gimpy charged like he was coming through the metal wire to shred me, howling like a banshee. He flipped over and over, legs flailing, teeth bared. I covered the trap with a sheet, which he tried to rip apart as I carried it to my car.

"He's a wild one," Jamie said. "You're not going to hurt him, right?" I promised he'd be fine and took him off to the Best Friends shelter a half hour away. There the assessment person decided in about one second flat that Gimpy was *not* going to be adopted as a lap cat, right about the time Gimpy tried to take *his* hand off.

The vet cleaned out his ear and gave him antibiotics for the infection, but the damage was permanent. Gimpy still walked sideways with a tilted head. The vet said Gimpy was eight months old and feral as hell, and that he should be put back on the streets with the other ferals.

That was a possible death sentence, as all across the city dog packs were hunting and killing cats, but there were hardly any places to send ferals outside of New Orleans. Even tame cats rescued from the city were being killed in some overcrowded shelters when they weren't adopted fast enough. And donated cat food was constantly in short supply for the cats still roaming the streets, which depended on an ever-dwindling number of volunteers to feed them all across the city. I had to arrange Gimpy's way out of this desolate hell. He didn't even have the chances another cat would, crippled the way he was.

A feral cat rescuer I knew agreed to take a few dozen cats to her sanctuary in North Carolina, including my little Gimpy. I warned her he was a hard core feral, but she didn't quite believe me ... until he arrived. After their first encounter she promptly renamed him Taz, for Tasmanian devil, after he tried to shred her into bite-sized morsels. He leaped at her, hurling himself against his crate, growling and hissing whenever she passed by. A feral cat expert, she rated Taz up there among the most feral cats she'd encountered. He had only two things on his mind: blood... and *her* blood.

But things slowly changed, and in a few weeks he was grabbing—not to attack, but for attention. One day Taz escaped from his kennel, and his life turned around. He began playing with the other cats at her home; he'd swat playfully at people, chase her around, and then grab her legs, riding on her jeans. He started jumping up to the kitchen counter when she prepared meals. When he lay in her arms purring, his belly up to be rubbed, she knew he wasn't the Tasmanian devil any longer.

Dogs are easy to gauge. Cats are difficult. They are complex and untrusting creatures, often misunderstood. But once you've earned their trust, they let you know. It's just a matter of earning it, not expecting it to be given automatically.

In New Orleans right now, thousands of cats are roaming the streets; they are afraid to come near people, just as untrusting as Taz was, just as frightened, yet they too could be as loving, if only they'd get the chance to have a home and someone to take care of them.

A resident who stayed behind with her pets leaves once police assure her she could take them in a transport. Many residents stayed in New Orleans without electricity or tap water for weeks to guard their animals.

Photo: Liz Roll/FEMA

Chapter 47

Left Behind to Live

I t was common knowledge among Gulf residents that pets would be safest if secured before citizens evacuated. For years these residents had heard that pets, scared by the howling winds and sheeting rains, might run and be lost forever. The owners were warned that pets would jump out of windows and be severely injured by broken glass. Or that flying debris would burst *in* through the windows, fatally wounding pets.

With this in mind many residents caged or crated their pets. Others confined pets in bathrooms, back bedrooms, even windowless garages, believing this would protect them. Others chained their pets outside. This would eventually lead to the death of many beloved animals.

Since rescuers were alone searching entire developments, heavily secured houses were usually passed up as too time consuming to break into. Homes boarded up with wood over every window were easily passed by, as many assumed no pets would have been nailed up inside. (We were dead wrong.) Homes heavily striped with thick iron security bars over all doors and windows were usually skipped. Unless there were telltale signs the owner might have pets, such as a doghouse outside, pet bowls, or animal figurines in window, the home was rarely entered. Any pets inside these secured homes were left behind. Even the expansive military and search rescue units had no time to break into every house. Yet you knew every time you walked away, you could be bypassing an awaiting animal, one that had heard you, then was left behind one final time.

Gulf residents will never forgive themselves for the pets left "safely" behind. Rescuers will never forgive themselves for the many mistakes we made and the countless houses passed by. I still wonder how many pets had waited silently inside, hearing us pass beyond their barred doors.

The one clear truth is that owners did not leave pets behind to die—the pets were left behind to live.

The following letter came to me from Sandra Bauer, an Internet reunion volunteer assisting Gulf residents from her home in Canada.

Karen,

Malvin and I have often wondered about Bandit and what happened to him after Malvin had to leave him. He might have been seen by someone like you, making his way from rooftop to rooftop, or through the mucky water that you were in, to safety, finally. They didn't all die … thank goodness. And those that did, they are at rest now.

Bandit

Photo: Sandra Bauer

There are many things that people did in the best interests of their animals that still resulted in the loss or death of their pets. Some people criticize Malvin for decisions he made, but when I reflect, he did everything right and that dog survived as a consequence. Thank goodness Malvin didn't lock Bandit "safely" inside the house, such as in the bathroom before he left, as his neighbor did—his neighbor's dog drowned, locked in that bathroom when twelve feet of water rushed into the neighborhood. Thank goodness Malvin didn't secure the porch door shut when he decided to place Bandit in the porch, which let out onto a (then) fenced yard. Thank goodness he decided instead to deliberately wedge the door open with a piece of wood so Bandit could come and go at will. "So he wouldn't be trapped," are the words Malvin used. Thank goodness he didn't tether Bandit in place. No leash, no tether, not under these circumstances.

He put plenty of food and water down for him and said, "I'll be back in a couple of days, Boo." (I imagine he said "Boo"—notice he calls Bandit "Boo" sometimes; sometimes he even calls me "Boo!") And when the torrent of water swamped the Desire neighborhood, Bandit was not locked inside because of these individual decisions that Malvin made, even while under the enormous stress of having to evacuate. Bandit probably swam through that awful water to the Lowe's hardware store on Elysian Fields Avenue a mile and a half away, from where he was eventually taken to Lamar-Dixon by individuals anonymous.

People criticize Mr. Cavalier for leaving Bandit behind, but he didn't have a choice. And under the circumstances, the decisions he made that day saved that sweet dog's life.

UPDATE: Bandit was rescued in New Orleans, then adopted out to a "new family" in Pennsylvania. It took a year, a lawsuit, and prominent media coverage before eighty-six-year-old Malvin Cavalier, Sr., would see his beloved dog again. After a final heartfelt plea from Mr. Cavalier, the new owners decided to do the right thing: They settled out of court and returned Bandit to his real home.

Chapter 48

Oops! I Stole That Dog

EXCERPT FROM AN E-MAIL
Subject: *Oops, I stole that dog...*
Date: *February 15, 2006*
From: *KO*

Hey there, got your message. What's with the dog on my lap? Good question. Well, I borrowed her. Okay, I out and out *stole* her.

That German shepherd was left out all day, tied to a fence in the pouring and freezing rain.

I first noticed her in the early morning. I was looking for kittens that had been abandoned under a house nearby and saw this dog tied up in a backyard. I remember thinking, *Cool*. The house was

177

newly painted, the owners were moving back in, cleaning up the yard, they had their pet tied out back for a moment. It was good to see that in New Orleans.

Later that night, *ten* hours later, after a drenching rain, an icy day, I returned to look for the kittens and there was the dog, *still sitting there*, tied up, wet and shivering. Her three-foot leash was tied so high up on the fence it left her only enough room to sit there pressed against the fence; there wasn't enough leash to let her lie down without hanging herself.

I banged on the door and a woman answered. I said, "This dog's been out here all day."

"No," she said. "She's been out there all month. Lives out there." The dog belonged to her sister but she told me her sister, now living at a friend's house, was too busy to come by. So, this lady explained, that she was stuck feeding the dog every morning at 6 a.m. before she left for work. (She fed him once a day in a shallow cat bowl.) But the bowl was upside down, out of the dog's three-foot reach. And I'm looking at the dog and she's just shivering—shaking, with those big sad eyes.

We got her sister on the phone and she didn't want any help. Kept saying it's *"my dog"* and that *"my dog* is fine." She said she had the dog tied to a pipe but there was a gas leak, so she moved her. You could smell the gas leaking everywhere. The sister on the phone refused all help. We called the gas company for them— I mean, it was a *huge* gas leak.

I came back the next day to check on the dog and this time the dog was tied to the broken pipe and the gas was still pouring out. We started the whole scenario again. I knocked on the door, the lady answered. We called the sister. Sister doesn't want help. I got nowhere.

Once the lady closed the door, I called around to control officers I'd met, but no one could get there. They all said the same thing, off the record: "Take the dog." *You know* I was gonna anyway. I untied the leash and ran off with her.

First I ran down the street in front of the house and hit a dead end full of rubble and broken glass. I had to turn around and run back *past* the house (the crime scene) again with my borrowed dog. I ran down the street, past Nancy, and around the corner. Nancy was parked out front of the dog's house waiting for me. She'd dropped me off so I could check on the dog and that was the last thing she knew. Now she sees me running up and down the street with a dog, not realizing that I stole the dog. She had no idea *what* I was doing. So now I'm waiting around the corner for the getaway car and it's not coming. We were parked right in front of their house with ANIMAL RESCUE, and a phone number written all over the car.

Finally I run to the car—in *front* of the house, *again*, with the dog, and knock on the car window.

Nancy asks, "What are you doing?" A good question, since now she's seen me running up and down the street in the dark all night. The whole thing wasn't very James Bond, but we rescued that dog.

Only now there was nowhere in town to take him. We called rescues and fosters, told them we needed a safe house for the night. We hid the dog away, took her to Algiers to the LA-SPCA the next day. The dog was so skinny her knees were bony and disfigured from long-time malnutrition.

Once at the shelter, the dog was put in a special row for abuse cases, and I was told it would take months for her case to come up. Thus for months she would be stuck in a 5' x 5' pen. You know that wasn't gonna happen!

As we looked for a foster home to hold her until court, the owners (AKA dog robbery victims) got involved. They paid all the fines and began animal care classes, realizing how poorly they had treated her. It was a huge turnaround for the owners—something you rarely see. Oh, but what a love that dog was.

Photo: www.lifeexposedphoto.com

A rescued dog clings
to a volunteer.

Chapter 49

Post-Traumatic Stress in People and Pets

We all saw them, the dogs and cats cowering in the back of their cages, head down, listless. They resisted all interaction with pets in surrounding cages and cowered from their human caretakers.

Katrina survivors, rescuers, and pets were often so overwhelmed and traumatized by the aftermath of the hurricane that they developed severe cases of post-traumatic stress disorder (PTSD), a medically-recognized condition that occurs after extreme stress, such as war, natural disasters, and serious accidents. Katrina was all of those things. She created nonstop feelings of intense fear, horror, and helplessness.

To paraphrase a saying: "That which does not kill you will set you free." But for the humans and animals that lived through Katrina, her memories may never set them free.

A Survivor Speaks...

Photo: Win Henderson/FEMA

Chapter 50

Have You Seen Timmy?

By Linda Walker, Survivor

I have been in counseling for post-traumatic stress disorder and the one thing that has always haunted me is the guilt that I feel over my animals. My therapist, an animal person himself, told me he did not like it when I did that to myself and told me to stop doing it; but the one thing you can never, never get out of your mind is the last time you held your animals and saw those little faces looking at you.

I could not say morning prayers for weeks because every time I said them I was on the sofa and Timmy, my Yorkie, would come and I would pick him up and put him next to me. The last morning we were together, he was high up on the bed ... the water was rising and he chose to jump off that bed and swim over to me—that little thing—and I picked him up. He was all wet and smelling from the water that was already beginning to have an odor and he sat next to me as I read the prayers. That is a memory that will never fade nor will the memory of when I kissed him and he was so happy and excited and turned his little head toward me. He had no idea, but I did know what was happening.

The cats, they were not as trusting. They knew from the beginning that things were not right, because they were mad that there was water all over and they could not get down off the mantle and table where they were. Those are memories that will never leave you, no matter how many times you hear people telling you that you had no choice.

Linda Walker 2-3-07

Timmy is still not home where he belongs, but I am still searching for him and if I find him I am prepared to do everything it may take to get him back. I will happily attempt to move heaven and earth to bring that special little dog home. He is my "heart" and I know I am his "heart," too. I am sure he misses me as much as I miss him. The search will continue—closure will only come to me when I know where he is, what happened to him. And hopefully once again he will be in my arms. Have you seen Timmy?

Chapter 51

Happy Tails

Before

Seven weeks after Katrina, I was asked by returning Katrina survivors to enter their apartment, as they feared finding their dog dead inside. Their dachshund mix was locked in their bathroom, cowering behind the toilet. At only four pounds, one forth her normal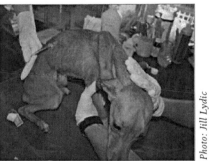

weight, the vet believes the only reason she survived was because there was so little room to move, she conserved energy. Sickly and dying, she was surrendered; her owners believed she wouldn't last much longer.

After

This loving, energetic, squirrel-chasing dog was renamed Shoog and lives with an animal rescuer in Florida. Shoog is now physically healthy but emotionally scarred. She is deathly afraid of being alone and cries incessantly when left

behind. "In fact," laughs the owner, "if I just put my shoes on or open a door, she panics."

Before

Jambalaya was one of only nineteen survivors rescued from Hell House, a suburban home with more than one hundred dead cats and dogs inside. Locked in the moldy, flooded house for five weeks without food and water, this cat was barely alive. He suffered severe respiratory problems and was covered with chemical burns, fungus, and open wounds.

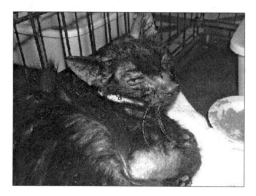

After

Today Jambalaya is a plump, happy feline described by owners as a "Velcro Kitty," since he's stuck on human contact. A big purr baby, he lives in North Carolina. Except for his fear of water, he's a happy, healthy, well-adjusted kitty.

Photo: Kristina Rieck

Before

Even today lost animals in New Orleans have little chance of survival in the empty city. This emaciated dog, named No Chance, was found behind a business in LaPlace, LA. The business owner called animal control and the dog was taken to the local shelter. As with all pets, the crowded shelter could only hold him for five days before euthanizing him. They hoped a rescue group would save him, as he couldn't be adopted out to the public due to restrictions on adopting pit bulls and pit mixes.

Photo: Jack Quick

After

ARNO stepped in and renamed this survivor *Chance*, giving him just that—a much deserved second chance. Within a month he was on the recovery, gaining sixteen pounds and doubling his weight. His blood work was perfect and he was started on heartworm treatment. He's a sweet, playful boy—and madly in love with the office cat.

Photo: Jack Quick

Photo: Jocelyn Augustino/FEMA

With sleep-deprived rescuers lacking cages and supplies, pets often came into rescue camps sharing unmarked cages. As street signs were down and houses underwater, documenting an animal's home address was often impossible. Surviving Katrina was their first miracle, finding their way back home would be miracle number two.

Chapter 52

The Tangled Web for Katrina Survivors

Internet reunion volunteers working all over the USA, trying to find missing Gulf pets, were dealing with victims—people who had not only lost their pets but every recognizable sign of their normal lives. They weren't merely displaced and traumatized; their worlds had vanished, replaced by a devastating new reality.

Within this newfound hell, they searched for their missing pets. That alone—losing your pet—for a person living a normal life is enough to cripple you emotionally. For Katrina survivors, this was one more piece of the dramatic puzzle. These people had no idea where to look for their pets and no reserve strength or mental capacity to do so.

To expect them to get on the Internet and search through records wasn't possible for most. Even if they had computers, even if they had electricity and Internet connections, many barely had the energy to search for their pets. Most owners were now homeless, living in new cities, overcrowding their relatives, sardined into tiny apartments, moving from couch to couch, trailer to trailer, city to city. Survivor Dana Liebert moved twenty-two times in the year after Katrina.

Yet the HSUS (which is not a government agency, nor affiliated with local Humane Societies), put out a nationwide alert stating that by December 15, 2005, all unclaimed Katrina pets nationwide could be adopted out to new homes. This gave displaced owners only three and a half months after the disaster to find their pets.

I heard the same story from many survivors: with no possessions, no computers, no homes, they would go to the local library in their new town, and were given one hour on the Internet. Most said experienced the same thing—they cried so much during their one-hour search online, that they couldn't see the keyboards. There they would sit, incapacitated, in plain view of a room full of strangers, sobbing at the library computer—knowing their one-hour window was closing fast and they were losing time. Or they had to rely on already busy friends, neighbors, and relatives to search the Internet for them. Many Katrina evacuees were unfamiliar with the Internet and this was no time to learn.

Yet the same system put in effect to save their pets would become the enemy. In many cases, after lengthy Internet searching, Web experts would track down a pet to a shelter only to be told they were "too late, the pet had been adopted out." One Humane Society questioned the sincerity of the owner to find their pet, saying that since the owner "had received $2,500 from FEMA, why hadn't they used the money to buy a computer and look for their pet earlier?"

But having the use of a computer wasn't the answer to many problems. Rescue paperwork—or more often the lack of paperwork—was the real nightmare. Many pets had escaped from their homes and were picked up roaming the streets. With no ID, they were brought into rescue outposts with no information. Paperwork might only say: *Black cat found on Haynes Boulevard.* The cat could be from anywhere, miles from its home, and worse, end up shipped anywhere in the USA. Street signs were down or gone. Rescuers were rushing, miswrote the paperwork, wrote no paperwork, left no message at the house, lost the paperwork. Confusing matters even more, with few cages, pets were often put together in the back of pickup trucks. As rescuers, living on the streets ourselves, we were on chronic overload.

Understandably, the mistakes made by sleep-deprived volunteers were many. Countless pets arrived at rescue centers with no information to follow them through the labyrinth of national shelters, making it impossible for owners to find them. Think about it: How do you find the love of your life if she/he, for example, is a medium-sized brown dog now somewhere in the vast United States? How do you find your adored black cat, gone, sucked into the world of shelters, foster homes, rescue groups, or individuals' homes? Or is your pet still on the Gulf streets, lost? Where do you begin?

Shattered Gulf residents gave us all kinds of details to help find their pets. When looking for a typical tan, medium-sized dog shipped somewhere in America, a frustrated owner told me to "throw a ball and he will jump straight up once before chasing it; that's how you'll know him." With millions of dogs in the country fitting the description of her dog, obviously this wasn't an option. And once again a pet was lost somewhere in America, swallowed up by the system.

When some Katrina survivors were told to go to Pet Finder, an Internet site, to look for their lost pets, they jumped at the chance. "I'll drive there right now!" a woman said. "Tell me what street it's on." *That is how little some knew about the Web.* In response, Stealth Volunteers and other Internet experts all over the world got involved and were instrumental in aiding Katrina survivors.

Ten days after Katrina this man had to be convinced to evacuate. He agreed to leave New Orleans only if his dog could stay with him.

Chapter 53

If you believe pets were abandoned on the Gulf, you don't live on the Gulf...

It was a year after Katrina and I was in a pet food store, in line behind a woman who clung proudly to her black and white papillion like he'd just won first prize in a dog show. "I don't care what happened," she continued telling the clerk, "I would never have left him behind. No way. Nothing could have stopped me."

I glanced down at the checkout counter and among the cans of pet food and the floral bandana she was buying was a pet magazine with Katrina on the cover, marking the first anniversary of the storm.

"You weren't on the Gulf, were you?" I asked.

"I didn't have to be there. I know how I feel about my dog. I would never leave him behind. Never!"

There's a lot we need to understand about the people and the pets of the Gulf. It's a complex, far-reaching issue. And it took a while for some of us on the ground, the rescuers, to understand.

At first, it was hard to feel sympathy for some pet owners in New Orleans. The amount of death and the horrific ways so many animals died angered many. Often dogs were found in their backyards, chained to the fence without a chance of survival. We'd find them locked in tiny bathrooms, tied to the doorknob, hanging. Pocket dogs and cats were found drowned or starved in small travel carriers where they were left, with barely enough room to turn around.

The stories are endless. I remember the backyard with four dead cocker spaniels, each tied to tree trunks by a few feet of linked chain. One cocker died with his head held high, which I couldn't figure out at first. Then I realized he died trying to keep his head above water and just froze like that, drowned, at the end of his short chain. Inside the living room of another house I found five dogs dead, each one alone, locked inside a cage far too small for its size. All had starved to death, none drowned; the water hadn't entered this second-story room. We saw this type of "abuse" all day, everywhere. It was a city ripped from the pages of a horror novel, from a sick imagination gone wild.

As hard as it was for some rescue and relief workers to understand, these residents loved their pets and thought they were protecting them. Dogs that lived outside were kept outside in "their homes," the backyards they lived in, and chained so they would be safe, so they couldn't run away and get lost. Pets were locked in small rooms, closets, and bathrooms so they would be safe from flying glass. For others left in cages, the owners believed their scared pets might run through the plate glass windows and get hurt, lost, or die.

For rescuers inside the city, with no TV, no radios, no real contact with the outside world, many of us didn't have the whole picture. But the truth slowly revealed itself.

Residents of the Gulf have gone through the hurricane drill ten times in the last seven years. It's something they live with. The norm. The routine. Sometimes they stay behind and wait for the storm. Sometimes they leave town. Most have learned that leaving town is not a great option. The roads are packed in stand-still traffic, gasoline prices escalate, hotels are booked, roadside restaurants are full, gas station restrooms have long lines. If you think rush hour traffic in any city is bad, imagine the traffic when an entire metropolis evacuates. And for evacuees, every hurricane warning for years had been a false alarm. Frustrated Gulf residents would fight their way out of town, only to fight their way back in again, days later, and no hurricane arrived.

For hurricane-jaded Gulf Coast residents, the approaching Katrina was no different. "Here we go again." Katrina was another drill. Those who evacuated thought: I'll pack up, safeguard my animals at home, leave—and be back in two days. And they were right; Katrina did little harm to the city. She had come and gone without much fanfare—until the levees broke. Suddenly these safeguarded animals weren't safe at all. They were unknowingly set up for failure. Unwittingly set up to die.

The flood changed the whole scenario. "I'll be back in two days" became "I couldn't get back for six weeks." Pet owners fought to enter their own cities. Those of us inside New Orleans were stunned by the great injustice. "The only people not allowed in the city," we'd say, "are the residents, the people who belong in the city."

Some owners took their pets with them when they evacuated. Many secured their pets in their homes before they left, and others were forced by authorities to leave their pets behind. Still other residents stayed in New Orleans *because* of their pets. When the levees broke, many people who had stayed behind to protect their animals would now die trying to save them.

As rescuers we had no time to remove the bodies of dead animals, no matter how or where we found them. We moved quickly to the next house in search of the living. Gulf residents who lost everything, who were already consumed with the guilt of leaving their pets behind, would return home to find their animals dead in cages, bathrooms, or still locked in the master bedroom, decomposing in their owner's bed. It was common to find cats curled up dead in their litter boxes, as if they sought final refuge in an enclosed, safe place. Katrina slammed right through the heart of many families when they realized they would never see their pets again, when they realized the suffering their pets experienced. Gulf residents will endure this loss and see the images of their dead animals for the rest of their lives.

I'll never forget the elderly woman who stopped me on the streets weeks after Katrina. As she spoke, she nervously rubbed the small gold cross dangling from the thin chain around her neck. "Please, can you help me? I live here, down the street. I left my dog in the garage. I left lots of food and water. He's a German shepherd. Could you, could you look? I left the city late. I live alone. Just me and him. I don't drive anymore. I wasn't gonna leave. My neighbors had a spot in the backseat for me. But they couldn't take him. Will you look in my garage? I'm sure he's okay. I left plenty of food and water. He's okay, right?" She stopped for a moment and gathered herself before she spoke, "He's my soul mate."

I looked in her garage. Her soul mate had drowned; his long leash, left to secure him, had wrapped around a pole as he probably swam in the high waters. The elderly woman had now lost the last thing, the only thing, that mattered to her.

I gazed up at the woman in the checkout line at PetSmart. "You had to be there to understand what really happened. Every case was different. You can't know unless you lived it. You may have *had* to leave your dog."

"I wouldn't leave him," the woman replied, the silky papillion still crushed to her chest.

I thought back to all the people who died trying to protect their pets and all the people who will be scarred forever due to the loss of their pets—and I remember when I thought the same way this woman did. Back when I first arrived on the Gulf. It seems so long ago. So, so long ago.

We Can Make a Difference

On October 6, 2006, President George W. Bush signed the Pet Evacuation and Transportation Standards Act (PETS). Never again will citizens be forced to leave their pets behind in a disaster. All states are required to present the Federal Emergency Management Agency (FEMA) with pet evacuation plans, or risk losing federal funds for emergency preparedness. FEMA is now authorized to provide assistance on local and state levels to help pet owners and create pet-friendly shelters.

"People victimized by disasters should not suffer needless additional injury by having to abandon their household pets or service animals to their fate," said representative Tom Lantos, a California Democrat who introduced the bill after viewing TV coverage regarding the case of Snowball. Snowball drew national attention when the media filmed this fluffy white dog being ripped from a little boy's arms as they boarded an evacuation bus. "This country needs the force of federal law to protect people in large scale emergencies who own household pets or service animals such as guide dogs," he continued. President Bush himself stated, "If he had to evacuate the one thing he would take would be his dog Barney."

Thanks to pressure from animal lovers nationwide, all states must be prepared to evacuate pets safely and efficiently. It's one of the very few benefits to arise from the wet ashes of Katrina.

Chapter 54

To the Rescue...

Rescue dogs helping man and their fellow animals

Before heading to the Gulf, these rescue dogs wait to be seen by a veterinarian.

Photo: Jocelyn Augustino

Rescue dogs can explore smaller spaces than their handlers.

Photo: Marvin Nauman/FEMA

Photo: Marvin Nauman/FEMA

This dog barks, alerting rescuers that he's picked up a human scent. Dogs are trained to lie down or bark to inform their handlers of a body.

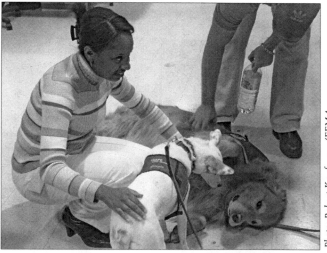

Photo: Robert Kaufmann/FEMA

Two of Hope Crisis Response's therapy dogs provide comfort to victims and relief units. Here they get attention from FEMA workers.

Part 3

KATRINA PET PROFILES

Photo: Dana Liebert

Chapter 55

TOBIAS, the Shih Tzu

AGE: 3½ yrs.

GENDER: Male

BREED: Shih Tzu

HOMETOWN: Meraux, Louisiana

NICKNAMES: Bubby, Mr. Happy

PERSONALITY: Friendly, courageous. Wasn't afraid of anything. A happy, people-oriented companion. Always wagged his tail.

FAVORITE TOY: His rubber duck collection. When asked where his baby duckies were, he'd race to gather all three, one at a time. Each hidden in its own secret place.

LIKES: Sticking his head out a moving car window. He'd jump into anyone's car to go for a ride. He loved shredding Kleenex and pulling Dana's hair bands from her ponytails. Often seen jumping on the couch, barking at noises. His motto was: Bark first, investigate later.

199

DISLIKES: Whenever his girlfriend, Zoe, the other Shih Tzu at home, stole his toys, Tobias whined like crazy. But he was too sweet to challenge Zoe. He panicked, hated when she stole his rubber duckies.

LAST SEEN: Dana was born and raised in Louisiana. She might leave up to three times yearly during hurricane warnings. She was overly cautious of impeding storms. But hurricane evacuation is no easy task. Items are carefully chosen and packed. A distant home or hotel had to be arranged. Work and schedules are interrupted. Wages lost. Money spent. And worst of all, the traffic. When more than a hundred thousand people evacuate at once, roads are bumper to bumper and gas is hard to find. Yet for Dana's family, the evacuation results were always the same. The hurricanes dissolved before touchdown and the family would drive home once again. This time they made a fatal error. They stayed.

Dana rode the storm out at her parent's two-story house. Katrina seemed no worse than any other hurricane and left the homes in her area unscathed. With no warning, on Monday, August 29, the living room door burst off its hinges, unleashing icy, raging salt water from the ruptured Forty Arpent Canal. Water engulfed the family. While Dana grabbed Tobias and her mother grabbed Zoe, the family climbed into the attic.

Cramped in the damp crawl space, unseen and unheard by neighbors, they waved a cheerleading pom-pom out the porthole window. Success. A passerby loaded the family and their pets in his boat and maneuvered them through the swirling waters to Chalmette High School. Soon they would all wish they had stayed in the attic. The high school was swarming with parrots, dogs, cats, and over one thousand frantic, traumatized victims. Many were barefoot and wore only pajamas or the underwear they escaped in. Most had no possessions at all.

The icy water had flooded the gym. People slipped in the oily mud. Some broke bones, suffered cuts, bruises, sprains.

Conditions worsened as diabetic patients without proper food or medicine weakened. A few of the elderly had oxygen tanks, but with no electricity to use them the chilled gym air exacerbated their conditions. "Man down!" was heard over and over as people passed out around the room. The gym had become a death trap. Surviving on looted donuts and soda, all waited to escape. But the situation deteriorated quickly over the next three days. With no toilets, survivors had to urinate in their own wet clothing. Sores developed on their legs and feet. Dana prayed for the people she heard had died among them in the gym.

Finally word came. The police allowed them to leave. By Wednesday morning, survivors marched through the chest-high waters of St. Bernard Parish. Authorities warned that if they took their pets now, they would be forced to let them loose on the levee. Dana decided it was safer to leave them behind, with the understanding that Zoe and Tobias would be cared for at the local jail.

Dana last saw Tobias when she held him at the gym. "Tobias," she said, "I have to leave you with Zoe. Take care of her, make sure she's safe." Dana assured Tobias she loved him and watched him as she walked to the exit. "Tobias stared back," she remembers. "Sitting like a good boy, staying right there. He was a very good boy, obedient always." After a pause, she continued tearfully, "I never saw him again but he took care of Zoe to the very end. We found her weeks later. She was at Camp Lucky, a small rescue center set up in the field behind the school. That was my boy, my sweet little boy. He loved his Zoe. Saved her life. I knew he would."

UPDATE: Dana moved twenty-two times in the three years after Katrina, residing in Tennessee, Alabama, Louisiana, Texas, and Arkansas. After living in three different FEMA trailers in New Orleans, she finally moved into her refurbished home in Chalmette, Louisiana.

Tobias is still missing and still missed. In all the upheaval and the emotional rollercoaster of being a refugee in her own country,

Dana never stopped searching for him. Still working with volunteer research experts, she distributed several thousand reward posters to New Orleans workers, residents, and Mardi Gras crowds. With the reward at $3,000, she considered it a bargain to get Tobias back in her life. Even though Dana lost all her possessions, she knew the only really important things she left behind were her pets. Tobias was, and still is, one of the greatest loves of her life. Dana said tearfully, "I look forward to the day I die when I can see sweet Tobias. I never had children; he was my baby. I hope God lets me be with him again someday."

In his memory, Dana had a plaque engraved and placed on the chair at the high school where she held Tobias for the last time, before leaving him behind.

Chapter 56

MIDNIGHT, the Potbellied Pig

AGE: 4 yrs.

GENDER: Male

BREED: Vietnamese Potbellied pig

HOMETOWN: New Orleans, Louisiana

NICKNAME: Middy Boo

PERSONALITY: Sweet. Intelligent. Very gentle, but could be stubborn if he didn't get his way. Would communicate through grunts and moans, but after four years with him everyone knew exactly what he wanted. Very affectionate, would rub on you constantly to say hello.

FAVORITE TOY: He loved his mattress. He'd push it around to a perfect position in the backyard and sprawl across it. He also loved leaves. He'd spend a half-day gathering them up to make a nest and lay in the sun. At night he'd move to his mattress.

LIKES: Midnight was a "people person." Loved to be petted, scratched. Raised with three dogs, he thought he was a dog. He had everything but the bark. Wagged his tail like a puppy and loved to have his long tail braided. He enjoyed long walks. He'd often wander to the neighbors for a visit. They'd tell him to sit and he would sit. He loved vanilla wafer cookies.

DISLIKES: Hated lightning and thunder. Got scared by fast movement.

LAST SEEN: Homeowners Robert and his old friend Rick had lived in this home through the biggest hurricane to ever hit New Orleans, Hurricane Betsy, on September 9, 1965. Betsy destroyed the neighboring county, St. Bernard Parish, but Robert's home was untouched by her wrath. With yearly threats of hurricanes, he wasn't worried about Katrina. New Orleans hadn't flooded in his lifetime.

Katrina came and left on August 29, passing over Gentilly Woods, Robert's neighborhood. A windy, howling hurricane, he could hear "transponders popping, utility poles snapping, and trees breaking." Garbage pails and debris whizzed by his window. He watched in amazement as the wind picked up a neighbor's truck and flung it like a plastic toy.

Then suddenly—Katrina was gone. All was calm. There was no wind, just a mist of showers outside. With the house unscathed, the only damage left by the hurricane was a yard full of debris.

As they cleaned up the trash on the lawn, they noticed a stream of water surging down the street. Robert was puzzled. Katrina had gone ... but *now* the streets flooded? Strange.

The water was shallow but fast. A current so strong it ripped sewer tops off the pavement. With enormous pressure, water surged up the street. Something was deadly wrong, but he didn't know what.

Robert and his best friend, Rick, scurried to collect their animals.. First they opened the large cages in their backyard, releasing a pair of peacocks. With the water surging, they raced inside to save five more animals: Roxanne the Rottweiler, Angel, an American pit bull terrier, NN the rat, Tiny the ferret, and of course their pig, Midnight. Up on the roof with their pets, they had a clear view of the water. Now raging, it carried cars, trucks, trees, and lawn furniture.

With little time to react, they opened the two small cages on the roof, releasing the ferret and rat. As the dogs could swim, they'd be easy to take. But Midnight? At over one hundred pounds and afraid of water, he was safer for now if left on the roof. The men grabbed the dogs and scrambled down into the chest-high water.

Robert remembers crying as he left the confused pig on the roof. He never believed he would bond so strongly, never knew how loving a pig could be. The two men struggled with the dogs as they treaded water down the street. A few blocks later, they moved onto higher ground, a dry cleaning store on the main road, Chef Menteur Highway.

For the next few days, Robert would swim home, the water now over eight feet deep, to check on his cherished pig. Each time Robert returned, Midnight would squeal incessantly. But Robert would be forced to leave without her; he had no way to move her.

In a few days, Rick commandeered a small boat and maneuvered to the house. Parking the boat on the roof, he loaded Midnight and returned to the dry cleaning store. The ferret, rat, and peacocks were gone.

The store they camped in wasn't safe. It was a war zone, with looting, robbing, and gunfire all around. A block away, a man opened fire on an Army engineer and was shot to death by the National Guard. The corpse would remain there for days. (This is the same corpse that I, too, saw for many days, not realizing until this interview that Robert and Midnight were living in the building across the street from me when I first arrived in New Orleans.) Neither the hurricane nor the floods scared Robert, but the people did. Seemed like everyone was armed with knives, guns, or metal pipes.

For nine days, this unusual family would live at the dry cleaners, until Levee Board police sent them to a nearby interstate to be shuttled out. Told they could take their animals, the two friends grabbed their pets and trudged through the streets. Waiting five hours on Interstate 10, they were soon informed that they could not take their pets. Arguments ensued. Finally the animals were tied in the shade underneath the freeway and Robert was assured the pets would be picked up by the LA/SPCA.

Helicoptered out to Aurora, Colorado, Robert and Rick would live on an army base. Two weeks later, they got a ride to Robert's parent's house in Houston. From here they frantically searched for their pets, calling everywhere. With a three hundred dollar phone bill and hundreds of man-hours spent, they came up empty.

Contacting the rescue center at Lamar Dixon, they were referred to an Internet expert, a Stealth Volunteer named Deborah Harman.

CURRENT STATUS: After much work, Deborah was able to locate the pets through PetFinder, the online database of animals that need homes. Midnight was tracked down to a pig sanctuary in South Carolina. He was reunited with his owners on November 26, 2005. Upon return, Midnight was so happy to see his family he laid his head in Rick's lap and wouldn't budge for hours.

Angel, the pit bull, found in a shelter in Pittsburgh, Pennsylvania, was delivered back home on December 18. Rick and Robert both agree it was the best Christmas present they'd ever had. Angel raced to see Midnight, and Midnight grunted with delight. They are inseparable now.

The peacocks, rat, and ferret were never found. Robert's Rottweiler is still missing. He believes that whoever has her would never give her back as she was too sweet, too loving. He calls her "the most affectionate, gentle dog you could ever meet."

As Robert says, "You can replace about everything in your life, but your pets are irreplaceable. All so unique, you can never get another animal just like the one you had. A different one, sure, but never the same one. Never." Both men feel blessed to have these two pets back. Still grieving over Roxanne, Robert only hopes she is in "a good home, a loving home, with a family that appreciates her."

UPDATE: When I interviewed Robert for this pet profile, I already knew his beloved Rottweiler, Roxanne, was dead. Records show that in early September she was held for ten days at the HSUS rescue facility at Lamar Dixon, then "euthanized" for being "extremely aggressive." But as I listened to Robert glowingly recount her life, I was struck by how often he described her as sweet and affectionate. I realized, once again, how gentle pets that suffered the trauma of Katrina often reacted with aggression. And how often they were killed in our unforgiving system. (For more on Roxanne, see "Dog, Interrupted.")

The only remaining
photo of Roxanne.

Chapter 57

AMBER, the Cat

AGE: 9 yrs.

GENDER: Female

BREED: Tortoise shell, domestic shorthair

HOMETOWN: Gentilly, New Orleans

NICKNAMES: Boombi Cat

PERSONALITY: A chatty, conversational, outgoing girl. Every morning Cathy would say, "Amber, did you eat your breakfast? And Amber would reply a big meow… a yes," her owner laughs. "If I left Amber for a period of time, she'd talk up a storm when I returned, reprimanding me for leaving her."

FAVORITE TOY: Her favorite toy was her owner, Cathy. She loved to watch TV with Cathy.

LIKES: Chasing rubber balls. Cathy would throw the balls and Amber would race to retrieve them. Cathy bred terriers for over forty years. Whenever a mother dog was out of the whelping box, Amber would jump in the box and guard the puppies. She loved playing with puppies.

DISLIKES: Doorbells; she'd dive under the covers and hide.

LAST SEEN: The night before Katrina, Cathy was working at Gambino's Bakery, selling cakes and donuts to evacuating residents. Cathy herself planned to leave early the next day for Baton Rouge. But there was one small detail she hadn't figured on. One detail that was about to drastically alter many lives. There was no gasoline left in New Orleans. After work, she drove from station to station, but they were either closed, or out of gas.

At home, the TV blared of impending doom. Mayor Nagin and Governor Kathleen Blanco advised inhabitants to "get out of the city!" Katrina was now a "very dangerous hurricane and headed straight for New Orleans." Nagin announced that the Superdome would be opened for those who could not evacuate. But the news was confusing. Officials urged evacuation, but Cathy remembers other news—that storm surges would be fifteen feet high but the levees could only withstand thirteen feet; any overflow would be handled by the high-tech pumping stations around the city. Rather than head to the Superdome, she decided to stay home. Stay home with her only family: two cats, seven dogs, and a cockatiel.

Cathy was awake that night while "the wind howled, screamed, and carried on." But Katrina left as quickly as she came. Except for the loss of electricity, all seemed back to normal. Later that afternoon, Cathy heard clanging sounds. Running to the living room, she discovered water gushing into her house. In minutes she was up to her knees in the ice-cold Lake Pontchartrain.

Panicked, she grabbed her two Rottweilers and her miniature poodle and lifted them into the attic. Water rising quickly, she found her four Maltese terriers and hoisted them up too. Her two cats, Milo and Amber, were huddled together, meowing frantically on top of the massive birdcage. Cathy grabbed them and waded to the kitchen, placing them in the highest cabinet. With nowhere to put her bird, she left him in his home, a six-by-six foot cage.

But Katrina wasn't done with Cathy yet. The high, black water bubbled like a geyser through the attic floor around her. The saturated wood floor gave out and her dogs fell through. They were yelping and splashing as they treaded water.

Cathy was able to get her Rottweiler, Zena, back into the attic, but the others drowned. Cathy grieved alone in the attic; for days, in her mind, she would hear her cherished cockatiel die. The pretty feathered boy that always called to her: "Hello, my baby. Hello, my baby." Cathy had listened helplessly as he drowned and will hear his painful scream for the rest of her life. Her only solace was Zena, snuggled beside her, and the two cats safe in the kitchen. They were still alive. She could hear them meowing constantly. "Swim to mama," she yelled to them. "Come on, swim to mama." The panicked cats wouldn't budge, but they called out to Cathy for six days.

Cathy had lived with tragedy before. Newly married in the early seventies, her husband would soon die in a plane crash on June 24, 1975. Eastern Airlines, Flight 66, on a flight from New Orleans to New York. He perished with 130 others. With no children, Cathy settled into a quiet life; her only family was her beloved pets. "I worked all week at the local bakery," she said, "and spent most of my salary on treats and gifts for my pets. I was happy," she reminisces. "Going to work, coming home, watching TV, and taking care of my animals. That was my life. For me, it was all I wanted. I was so happy with my little life."

But Katrina would change all that. After six days in the attic, Cathy realized no one was coming for her. She swam out of the attic and dove down to try to open the front door, but the water pressure was too much. Among the floating furniture and household items in her living room, she noticed a bottle. Slamming it into a window, she made her escape.

Rescued by boat, she begged to go back for her pets, but no one would listen. Shuttled to higher ground to a nearby football field, a military copter would then fly her to the local airport, where she would be jetted to a shelter in Corpus Christi. Dressed in only a T-shirt and underpants, the military gave her clothing and immunizations. They offered her food, but Cathy remembers: "I didn't want food, I wanted my family. My pets. I begged them to take me home for my pets. That's all I ever wanted. I will never forgive myself for leaving them behind. I should have stayed with them."

Cathy then lived at a friend's house in Oklahoma City. She didn't return to New Orleans for four months. Four long months of sorrow over her lost family. Upon return to New Orleans, Cathy was warned by animal rescuer Judy Swartwood not to enter her home, knowing the sight of her deceased pets would be overwhelming. The Catholic Charities organization retrieved her dead family and held a memorial service for them. Her cats, Ruben and Amber, were gone (they had been rescued) but Zena, her beloved Rottweiler, is still lost somewhere in the United States. Zena was a "two-year-old female with beautiful teeth and had her dewclaws on all four feet. If anyone knows her whereabouts, please contact me."

Rueben is now more spoiled than ever. As for the chatty cat, Amber, she's settled back into life with Cathy. She sleeps on Cathy's pillow every night, purring away. Amber's new favorite pastime is reaching up and smacking Cathy's new red poodle in the head. As soon as Amber gets a slap in, she jumps up on the windowsill out of the dog's reach. Cathy swears she's smiling up on that windowsill.

And once again, Cathy spends most of her weekly salary buying treats and gifts for her pets. Just like the good old days.

Chapter 58

JACK, the Cockatiel

AGE: 15 yrs.

GENDER: Male

BREED: Gray cockatiel

HOMETOWN: New Orleans, Louisiana

NICKNAME: Jack

PERSONALITY: Jack was born a small, scrawny cockatiel. His weak, timid nature alienated his cage mates. Often alone, Jack developed a relationship with one bird that was *always* there for him. That bird was Jack, himself. Jack fell in love with his own image in the mirror.

FAVORITE TOY: Any mirror.

LIKES: Rubbing on the perch and admiring his reflection, or singing and bobbing to music.. Jack loved to mimic Connie as she danced playfully for him while vacuuming. He enjoyed getting out of the cage to ride on the back of Dixie, the family's poodle mix. He *loved* Doritos and potato chips.

DISLIKES: Being picked on by other birds, he would retreat to the bottom of the cage.

LAST SEEN: Expecting to be out of town for three days due to Katrina, Connie Miller, her husband Eric, and a neighbor's son loaded up their four small dogs and headed off to a relative's home in New Albany, Mississippi, three hundred miles northeast of New Orleans.

Boarding up the house, they left their three cockatiels and their parrot, Rambo, locked safely in their cages. This wasn't the first time they would evacuate for a storm. The Millers packed up everything for Hurricane Ivan but awoke the next morning to discover their trailer, their possessions, even their motorcycle had been stolen out of the driveway. And Ivan never arrived.

Once Katrina left and the levees broke, the Millers were in a panic to get home, believing they were close enough to easily return for their birds. But they would soon discover that three hundred miles away might as well have been three thousand, because for the Millers, as for most Louisiana residents, New Orleans was an impenetrable city. Four times, they attempted to get into the city, to save their birds, but were turned back by police, military, and roadblocks. This was a common problem and frustration for residents. Local TV news blared incessantly that the city was closed down and no residents were allowed back. Yet to evacuees, it seemed everyone was allowed in their city—except them.

After a few weeks, New Orleans was crawling with Red Cross, utility workers, debris removers, animal rescuers, Mexican laborers, and reporters. "But these were *our* homes, *our* property, *our* pets left behind," Connie states. "And our hands were tied." Anger and frustration mounted for evacuated residents. For Connie, images of her birds struggling, perhaps starving, were constantly on her mind. Soon fuel shortages spiked prices and gas was rationed. In many areas of Mississippi, patrons were only allowed to pump ten gallons at a time. The Millers feared they would run out of gas on the road into New Orleans.

Four weeks later, after Hurricane Rita had come and gone, the Millers attempted to cross Highway 11 once again. Driving as far as Metairie, only ten miles from their house, they were turned away. Finally a friend gave Eric Miller official documents to help him get through, but police refused to even look at the paperwork, sending him back again. Mayor Nagin began allowing residents back in by zip codes, area by area, depending on how much damage was in each zone. Living between two main breached levees, the London Canal and the Industrial Canal, it would be six weeks before the Millers were permitted to return home.

Their house destroyed, their birds missing, the Millers began a frantic search for their cockatiels and their parrot Rambo. Connie thought of each one of them: Rambo, her affectionate Mama's boy; Whitey and Pearl, her bossy, independent cockatiels; and of course her precious little Jack. Her scrawny little mama's boy that needed special attention and a mirror to feel safe. But amidst all the sorrow, there was good news. On Thanksgiving, they heard a soft meow issue from under a neighbor's house. Connie kept calling until a traumatized feline peeked out. It was the friendly outdoor tabby that had previously become part of the Miller's family. After a month of hiding and cowering, the tabby recuperated from the emotional damage of Katrina and became her playful, loving self once again.

With no home, the Millers were soon living in a trailer park. Connie spent all her days on her laptop using the Internet with a data card. The Millers were fortunate; most residents had lost their computers, electricity, phone service, and Internet access, leaving them unable to search for their pets. Many residents of the area had no experience using the Internet at all and were incapable of researching their lost pets.

Connie amassed a database of contacts for shelters, rescue centers, and bird sanctuaries. After many false leads, she called yet another number, reaching Donna Powell. In the months after Katrina, Donna's house in Baton Rouge became a trauma center where hundreds of large parrots, cockatiels, and parakeets would find shelter. As Connie described her Amazon parrot on the phone, she mentioned his name, Rambo.

"Stop right there!" Donna said. "I have him. He says his name all the time. He keeps repeating: 'Hi, Rambo. Hi, Rambo.' "

Yet Connie's other cockatiels were not there. Cockatiels are harder to find. Often gray or white, with no outstanding characteristics, they all look similar.

After months of searching, Connie lost hope. Perhaps her beloved birds were dead or lost forever in the expansive nationwide system. After many frantic posts on the Internet, Connie all but gave up.

CURRENT STATUS: Three months later, out of the blue, Sandy Pellegrine, a Stealth Volunteer from Massachusetts, e-mailed Connie with new hope. She informed Connie that she might have found the birds over the Internet. And indeed, she had.

Connie and her birds are all a family once again. Little Jack is happier and stronger than ever. The ugly duckling blossomed after this experience. While lost, a vet diagnosed him with fatty liver disease and he was given a new diet and medication. Now he is as big and strong as the others.

Once again Jack is singing and bobbing to the music and the vacuum. And every once in a while he goes off his diet to eat his favorite food, Doritos. But mostly Jack spends his time proudly admiring that big, handsome hunk in the mirror—himself.

Chapter 59

MAX, the Dachshund

AGE: 2 yrs.

GENDER: Male

BREED: Miniature dachshund

HOMETOWN: St. Bernard, Louisiana

PERSONALITY: Full of life and play. A blizzard of activity. You'd think he had a list of things to do; only time he stayed still was at night in bed.

NICKNAMES: Max, Maxi

FAVORITE TOY: A squeaky orange ball he tried to tear apart. He was too small to destroy it, so he could only chase and squeeze it, but he never gave up.

LIKES: Wrestling with his fellow siblings—two dachshunds, Indie and Mocha Bean, plus a chihuahua named Rebel. He was fascinated by the new additions to the family: Indie's four newborn puppies. Loved stretching out upside down on Kit's lap watching TV and burrowing under the covers to sleep next to Kit and his siblings. He loved eating Bacon Bits, popcorn, Milk-Bones, and especially Fruit Loops.

DISLIKES: Piercing and ringing sounds like sirens and bells. He'd howl at passing ambulances and ice cream trucks. He disliked men. Growing up in a household with a woman, he was nervous around men.

LAST SEEN: Max's owner Kit had nowhere to go to escape the hurricane. No relatives to shelter her and no place to run with eight tiny dogs. She was alone in the house the morning of the hurricane, and Katrina was in high gear.

Kit awoke to discover water seeping under the front door. Sopping it up with a mop and newspaper, she realized the electricity was out. Gathering flashlights and candles for later, she settled into her recliner, the dogs piled in around her.

Suddenly she noticed water oozing beneath the front door again. Pulling open the wooden front door, the screen door exploded off its frame as water gushed in. Kit was waist-high in the icy Mississippi ... a raging whirlpool of water. Max and his petrified siblings cowered on floating chairs and couches.

In freezing murky water, Kit grabbed Max, yanked down the attic ladder from the ceiling, and raced up. One by one she waded through the icy waters to save her family of eight dogs.

At only 4' 11", Kit had to move quickly. Water was already up to her chest. After securing the dogs, she made one more trip down the ladder and swam to get dog food. She struggled to pull up the ladder as the water rose to the ceiling.

Alone in the attic with Max, Mocha Bean, Indie, Rebel, and the four puppies, she hoped to be rescued. Outside she could hear the occasional motorboat humming in the distance. But yelling out, no one could hear her.

Ten hours later, someone heard. A boat with three good Samaritans stopped. Kit passed her precious pets out a ripped metal vent and climbed out behind them. The group was taken to shelter at Beauregard Middle School. Kit wasn't alone there. More than seventy other survivors were gathered at the school. Dogs and cats were everywhere. Without food or water for three days, rescuers from the Wildlife and Fisheries Department came by, stunned that the school was a makeshift shelter. The rescuers took survivors by boat to local stores to salvage canned foods.

Kit made a bed out of a cardboard box in a schoolroom upstairs, but with more than one hundred pets running around she sheltered her babies in the adjoining smaller classroom.

Days later the water had receded and most of the group, with the exception of a few teens, were squashed into a dump truck and shipped out. Crossing the river by ferry, they were sent to various sites around the USA. Kit arrived in Muskogee, Oklahoma. Max and his siblings were *not* on the truck when Kit was forced to leave. Although she begged to take her dogs, local sheriffs demanded all pets be left behind. Kit was assured the dogs would be fed and kept safe.

With markers, Kit wrote notes on the wall outside the classroom where her dogs were to be watched, informing people of their names, breed, and sweet personalities. She thanked rescuers in advance for taking care of her precious dogs. Max was last seen when Kit went into the classroom to say goodbye and give him fresh water and Fruit Loops. She gave them all hugs and kisses and told them she would see them soon, promising they were in good hands, that kind rescuers would take care of them. But Max would not live to see her again.

CURRENT STATUS: Max and his siblings were found dead a week later upstairs at the school where Kit left them. Along with ten other dogs, he was shot at close range by a shotgun. While some speculate the local police did it in a scenario similar to the shootings across town at St. Bernard High School, others believe Max and the remaining pets were killed by local teens, or by volunteers who were tired of caring for the animals. The truth may never be known. Even with Pasado Safe Haven's $25,000 reward for information leading to a conviction, no one has stepped forward.

Kit is heartbroken to have lost her family and prays they died quickly and as painlessly as possible. She never returned to the school and has moved out of St. Bernard Parish.

On a happy note, Rebel, the chihuahua, was later found at a rescue center and was reunited with Kit.

NOTE: Although Kit loved all her dogs, she chose to highlight one, Max, as he was with her the longest. With waters twenty-seven feet high at her house, Kit lost everything. Not one possession remained. Not even a single photo of her beloved family: Max, Indie, Mocha, and the puppies. All that remains of Max is the note she left that fateful day on the middle school wall. That, and her undying love for him.

Chapter 60

SUGAR, the Poodle Mix

AGE: 12 yrs.

GENDER: Male

BREED: Poodle mix

HOMETOWN: Chalmette, Louisiana

NICKNAMES: Mr. Sugar, Little Guy, Sugs

PERSONALITY: A sweetie—a snuggle-bunny for Sharon.

FAVORITE TOY: His constant companion, Bubba, the Rottweiler, which he grew up with.

LIKES: To walk around the block with the family so he could bark at noises. He liked to spend time with the family and snuggle with Sharon. And he loved Milk-Bones—*really* loved Milk-Bones.

DISLIKES: Water. Chaos, loud noise. Hated vets and groomers. He would only go to the groomer if Bubba went first.

LAST SEEN: Sugar's owner, Sharon, stayed home through hurricane Katrina. Having been through twenty hurricanes or hurricane threats without damage in forty years, she felt secure staying put. Home with four other adults and two dogs, Sugar and Bubba, they rode out Katrina. Fast and furious, Katrina snapped trees, stripped tiles off their roof, and tore down fences. When the winds died, water crept up the driveway. Odd. The water came faster and faster. Chaos ensued. Sugar disappeared. Within minutes the family was up to their shoulders in water. No one knew where the water came from ... but it wasn't from Katrina.

Bubba was shoved out the window to escape, but Sugar was gone. The family barely made it out. They jumped through a window onto their van, which was bobbing against the house, and climbed on the roof. It took twenty minutes from the time the water flooded the driveway until the family and Bubba were on the roof. The last time Sharon saw Sugar, he was scared to death, running down the hall to hide under a bed. Once Sharon was on the roof, noting the water level around them, she believed Sugar had drowned.

CURRENT STATUS: When National Guard roadblocks allowed the family to return home a month later, they discovered that Sugar was gone. After searching the Internet and local neighborhoods for ten months, Sharon found his photo online. Sugar had been rescued from Chalmette and airlifted out of Louisiana with 125 other rescues. Luckily for Sugar, a good Samaritan named Joan was on the plane and noticed the emaciated, shaking Sugar collapsed in his cage. Fearing he wouldn't live through the flight, she pulled him from the cage and caressed him during the entire trip. Upon arrival in Florida she raced Sugar to her vet, saving his life.

Through phone and Internet contact, Sharon developed a steadfast relationship with the woman. Realizing the love and happiness in Sugar's new life, Sharon gave him to Joan. Sharon herself was still homeless, having moved seven times in four years after Katrina. Now living in a cramped one-bedroom apartment, she believed Sugar was better off with his new family. Sharon and Joan are still in touch today. And Sugar, as always, must have his daily Milk-Bones because he loves Milk-Bones—*really* loves Milk-Bones.

UPDATE: Almost five years after Katrina, I received an update from Sharon. Here's what she said about Sugar:

> **Subject:** RE: Hi Sharon
> **Date:** Thu, 1 Apr 2010
> **From:** Powers, Sharon
>
>   Sugar is still hanging in there. Isn't that amazing? He'll be 17 this year, and even though he is now completely blind and has developed skin issues, his spirit is still strong. I thank God every day that he was found by such a loving and caring person. Couldn't have asked for anyone better.

Photo: Amy Borne

Chapter 61

BARON, the Lab Mix

AGE: 9 yrs.

GENDER: Male

BREED: Lab & golden retriever mix

HOMETOWN: Chalmette, Louisiana

NICKNAMES: Buddy, My Boy

FAVORITE TOY: He loved to play with tennis balls. He'd push them around and if he thought no one was looking, he'd try to pick them up. *Only* if no one was looking. (He could be very private about certain things.)

LIKES: Nighttime walks with Amy's husband. And burying bones in his favorite hiding place, behind the air conditioning unit outside. Of course, it wasn't *really* a hiding place; everyone knew about it. He loved Kibbles and Bits and waited nightly for Amy's father to visit with table scraps.

DISLIKES: When the kids left for the bus stop in the morning, he would whimper and bark inconsolably.

LAST SEEN: Amy Bourne and her family packed up their compact car and left for Dallas two days before Katrina. Cramped for the long trip, they decided it best to leave Baron with her father, who had a van for evacuation.

Amy's father chose to ride the storm out, assuming that, like most hurricanes, this one would blow over. And he was right. Katrina caused their house little damage. But no one knew she was about to change history. When the canals and flood walls breached, millions of gallons of water came barging down the street.

Running through the neighborhood with Baron, Mr. Juneau, Amy's seventy-year-old father, raced to their local church. Built on higher ground, the church was a two-story building. As water flooded the first floor, Mr. Juneau protected Baron upstairs.

Passing boats refused to take the dog onboard. Boat after boat passed, unwilling to take Baron. Finally Mr. Juneau was assured that Baron would be well cared for at the church and be reunited quickly with the family. Reluctantly, Mr. Juneau climbed into a boat.

Baron was last seen wagging his tail at the church as the boat pulled away. Neither the dog nor Mr. Juneau took their eyes off each other until the boat turned a corner. This final image of Baron is painfully engraved in Mr. Juneau's memory. No one knew that this was the beginning of long, painful saga to reconnect with Baron.

CURRENT STATUS: Animal rescuers took Baron from the church to the LSU Veterinarian School, a holding site for pets. Here his paperwork misidentified him, making it almost impossible for the Bournes to trace him.

It took five months of exhaustive research to locate him. Stealth Volunteers finally tracked him down to the Arizona Humane Society. Although he wore updated rabies tags, for some reason the Humane Society did not contact the Bourne family.

Baron was adopted out and the Humane Society refused to give Amy the identity of the new owners, making it impossible for her to track him down. She was told, among other things: "He gets along too well with their three dogs."

The problem of "old owner vs. new owner" was a dilemma countrywide. Groups could not hold Katrina pets indefinitely, hoping that *maybe* their Gulf family would reappear someday. There had to be a cut-off. Once organizations readopted the pet, I found that they too often sided with the new family and would refuse to give any information to the Gulf owner. For me this was a bruising slap to already reeling Katrina victims, and the wrong thing to do, as these families would often work it out together. But lawsuits were flying, as new owners believed they were better homes for the "abandoned, sick" pets of the Gulf. Just like the original family, these new adopters were bonded with the pets.

Baron lived in Arizona before being moved to somewhere in the Carolinas.

The Bourne family had raised Baron from a puppy when they found him abandoned in the woods. They grieve his loss and believe that he too grieves for them. There is a lawsuit pending by the Attorney General of Louisiana to have Baron returned home.

UPDATE: Excerpt from an e-mail from Stealth Volunteer Susan, who worked for years on this case:

> Hi Karen,
>
> The woman who had Baron was identified and was then contacted by one of the attorneys from Best Friends. Amy was put in touch with the adopter and discussed in great detail the circumstances surrounding their separation during Katrina and his current health issues. After many conversations, although Amy had the opportunity to reclaim him, she and her husband selflessly decided it was best for Baron to stay put, versus uprooting him. The families continue to stay in touch. Susan.

RESOURCES

What's Happening in *Your* Local Pound?

Every year an estimated six million pets are dropped off in America's pounds. The owners kid themselves that someone will fall in love with their feline—or flip over their Fido. Sorry. Most years up to 70 percent of all animals in pounds will be killed. Over 56 percent of all dogs and a staggering 73 percent of all cats entering these facilities will not make it out alive. (Statistic according to the National Counsel on Pet Population Study, which adds, "only 23 percent of cats in pounds will be adopted, and only 2 percent reunited with their owners.")

The public acquires just 14 percent of its pets from shelters; 48 percent get their pets as strays or from friends or others, another 38 percent get their pets from breeders or pet stores. That's the reality. You can walk off and tell yourself that your pet will be one of the few saved, but chances are you will be dead wrong.

Animal care and control varies greatly across the USA. In one state your pet may be killed within seventy-two hours—in another, fourteen days. In some states your animal will be sold for research—in other states, it's illegal. In many regions, local authorities, cities, counties, parishes, or municipalities have jurisdiction over animal control, which can mean anything can happen, from having clean, caring, no-kill shelters to using gas chambers, heart sticks,* or even shooting pets, as occasionally backwoods pounds have been caught doing.

Another fate your pet may suffer is pound seizure, where it will be released for research and experimentation. While only two states insist, by law, that their pounds hand over animals to research labs, don't be fooled that your area is safe. Most other states allow each pound, or county, to decide whether or not they want to sell the pets in their care for experimentation. The true, honest numbers may never revealed, but according to the Foundation for Biomedical Research, over 140,000 dogs and over 50,000 cats annually will be sold for experimentation to be used for "acute, non-survivable" research.

Here's the state-by-state breakdown of pound seizure regulations.

MINNESOTA and OKLAHOMA mandate that any and all pound animals *must* be released to any licensed research facilities if so requested.

Eighteen states ban pound seizure: CA, CT, DC, DE, HI, IL, ME, MD, MA, NH, NJ, NY, PA, RI, SC, UT, VA, WV. (New York, Maryland and West Virginia prohibit the release of dogs and cats only—ferrets, rabbits, etc., are fair game. The other fifteen states listed here ban the release of *all* animals.)

Nine states allow their counties and individual shelters to choose whether or not to release animals for research: AZ, CO, IA, MI, OH, SD, TN, WI, UT. (Pets are not safe from experimentation in these states) Until recently, Utah, like Minnesota and Oklahoma, mandated that any and all animals must be given up upon a lab's request. In March 2010, Utah finally changed its law. While their pounds may still release pets for research, at least now they can make the decision, and are no longer in violation of the law if they do not.

Twenty-two states have *no laws* on pound seizure: AL, AK, AR, FL, GA ID, IN, KS, KY, LA, MS, MO, MT, NE, NM, NV, NC, ND, OR, TX, WA, WY. (Here too, these pounds have the right to sell pets for experimentation. To sell, or not to sell. That is the question—and in these states, shelters can answer however they please.

Any states that allow pound seizures, or have no laws regarding pound seizures, do sell their pets to both research labs and Class B dealers, who are often the middlemen for research facilities.

If you plan on leaving your pet at the pound, you should know what its death might entail. Or, you can kid yourself that someone will be dying to take your pet home—and you can walk away guilt free. Or at least *try* to walk away guilt free.

Again, how many people does it take to euthanize a pet? Two—someone to give the injection and one uncaring owner.

* I've mentioned heart sticks before; this is often a painful death. A needle containing sodium pentobarbital, a Schedule II controlled substance (also called "blue solution" or "blue juice") used to "euthanize" animals is slammed into the animal's chest cavity, going through several layers of muscle before puncturing the heart. Frequently no sedatives or pain medications are given first—and often the heart muscle is missed and the needle punctures the lungs, causing death by suffocation when the lungs fill with fluid.

The Surprising Chain of Events, and the Many Volunteers Involved, When You Don't Spay/Neuter

1) Your pet has a litter.

2) You may decide to keep some of the offspring, give some away, sell them, or take them to the pound. (Some people will dump them in nearby woods, deserts, or parks.)

3) If you give away any of this litter, and any of the animals were not spayed or neutered (S/N), you can be sure that some of this litter will create offspring. And some of this offspring, somewhere down the line, will end up in pounds. (From getting lost, to being dumped there, some *will* end up in pounds.)

4) Pounds are already full when this offspring arrives. Your "simple litter" is about to change the lives of many national volunteers, who will now have to work on weekends, or after their 9–5 jobs, or give up all their spare time to try (usually fruitlessly) to save these pets.

5) If the offspring are lucky, a volunteer with a camera will visit the pound to take photos of the pets stuck there. This novice **PHOTOGRAPHER** has the heartbreaking job of spending her (or his) free time inside pounds, knowing that most of the animals she is interacting with will be dead in a few days.

6) These photos will be sent to **INTERNET CROSS-POSTERS**. Cross-posters are volunteers who send animal information over the Internet to anyone who may have interest. That may be other cross-posters, Yahoo groups, friends, other rescuers— *anyone* who may be able to save the pet's life.

7) While an average of 70 percent of all these pets will be killed, let's say, incredibly, someone finds a **HOME** for one member of this litter. Often the newly found home is clear across the USA. Someone in Oregon might want the black Labrador (we'll call him Rudy) in a photo from a Mississippi pound—now it gets more difficult. (This cross-country homing is very common; what is not common is that a black Lab would be saved. There are too many black Labs and black cats in pounds; with this "undesirable" color, they are among the first to be killed.)

8) With all the work going into saving Rudy, rescuers will make sure they've found a good home. Over the Internet, word will go out that a **HOME VISIT** is needed. With luck, an Oregon rescuer will be found to check out Rudy's new family.

9) Now a **PULLER** must step in. The cross-posters will put out word that a "pull" is needed at the Mississippi pound. Hopefully, a local rescuer, with contacts at that pound, will pull Rudy out for free.

10) A **FOSTER HOME** is now needed—someone to hold Rudy until his transport is figured out. (Remember, all of these people are working for free to save Rudy.) If no local foster home is found, rescuers will spend their own money for BOARDING in Mississippi, just to get him out of the pound quickly.

11) Now **DRIVERS** get involved. The foster home will only keep Rudy a few days. If he's being boarded, he has to get out quickly, or rescuers will pay a fortune keeping him there. Truckers crisscrossing the USA, or rescuers traveling—*everyone* is asked to help transport Rudy some or all of the way. Usually, a **TRANSPORT COORDINATOR**, who will put this plan together and advertise for drivers online, works out "legs" of the trip. Rudy may get a ride from Jackson, Mississippi, to

Houston, Texas, then need many other legs of the trip to get him to Oregon. **OVERNIGHT HOMES** may be needed for Rudy along the way.

(If you're wondering why the new family doesn't pay for all this transport, boarding, etc., it's because they will often back out of the adoption, due to the expense. Meanwhile, rescuers want to get pets off death row—so they can't leave Rudy to die—when they've found a home. So everybody jumps in to save his life.)

12) It may take days, countless Internet pleas, and many volunteers' time, but Rudy will be delivered to his new home in Oregon.

Your "simple" litter created the need for:

A photographer
Cross-posters
A home visit
A puller
A foster home
Possible boarding
A transportation coordinator
Many drivers
Overnight stays
A new home

You may think: not any pets from *my* litter, someone local surely went to the pound and saved them. Most probably, a local volunteer or pound workers themselves did take photos. And the pet was posted on the Internet, and ... you know the rest of the story. If the pet was very, very lucky it was saved. But only one out of seven will be *that* lucky.

Please spay and neuter. Not only will you save lives, you will also help volunteers nationwide, so they don't have to spend their lives in the depressing world of America's pounds.

How You Can Help Save America's Pets Today

"Never doubt that a small group
of dedicated citizens can change the world.
Indeed, it is the only thing that ever has." —Margaret Mead

While rescues always need funding, there are many ways to help, like donating time, goods, and services. As you'll see here, you can save an animal's life by simply being attuned to the world around you. We can make a difference.

Pick a local rescue group you believe in and check it out in person. Get to know them. Are they no-kill? How are the animals cared for? How does their spay/neuter program work? Make sure that everything you donate works hard for the pets. There's everything from shepherd sanctuaries to rabbit rescues. (For a partial list of groups in your state: www.shelters.theanimalnet.com.)

Your Items Are Needed:

Dry or canned pet food & treats

Collars and leashes

Pet food coupons

Scratching posts

Animal grooming equipment

All office supplies

Office furniture

Humane traps (for catching ferals)

Doghouses

Kitty litter

Pet toys

Pet carriers

Medical supplies

All cleaning supplies

Postage stamps

Folding tables

Air miles

Doggie beds

For horses: salt blocks, hay, riding equipment, grooming items, etc.

Helping rescues and pounds can be a recycler's delight. Get rid of the clutter (as they say, clean your closets and you'll clear your mind).

Bedding materials are lifesavers in the winter, when many pound pets sleep on icy concrete floors or outside in snowy runs. Recycle old towels, linens, carpet remnants, fabrics—even that stale hay your horse scoffed at.

Remodeling? Rescues build crates, cages, runs. They may need everything you've got, including the kitchen sink.

Your Time Is Needed:

Spay/neuter. Spay/neuter. Spay/neuter. (No surprise I put that first.) Pet already fixed? Then S/N a friend's pet as a gift for a birthday or a holiday.

Got stray cats around? Local organizations will help you trap/neuter/return. (Check out www.alleycat.org)

Got a truck? Hauler? Rescues get donated items that need to be picked up and delivered.

Have your own garage sale; invite a rescue to join. Get help with the labeling and the sale—give them a percentage of the earnings.

Hold a book sale, bake sale or craft sale, inviting area residents to sell their wares, a portion to go to charity. (Call the local paper and get free publicity.)

When a rescue group is having an event—a walk-a-thon, silent auction, whatever—spread the word, tell your friends, tweet about it on Twitter, grab some buddies and go!

Animal groups schedule adoption events at national stores such as PetSmart, PETCO, and smaller regional and local pet stores. Libraries, churches, and parks might also hold adopt-a-thons. It's a great way to get out, meet people, and lend a hand.

Walk dogs at the pound. (Can't motivate yourself to exercise? Make a date with a pound dog.)

Play with cats. Some pounds and rescues have a cattery. Immerse yourself in a room full of furry felines, purring, rolling, rubbing on your legs ... or eyeing you with suspicion. If there's no cattery, cats stuck in individual cages need your time even more.

Foster cats, dogs, puppies and kittens. Especially in the spring, when litters flood the pounds. Nursing mothers will come into pounds, their babies too young to adopt, and the whole family will be killed. All they need is a space to lie down. The mother will take care of her own babies—how easy is that!

Heart set on a purebred pet? Check your pound first, where on average 30 percent of the animals will be purebred. Or Google it—there are hundreds of groups that have purebred rescue dogs. Same with cats, or try: http://www.purebredcats.org/rescues.htm; Email: Rescue@purebredcats.org

Never buy a pet from a puppy mill, pet shop, backyard breeder, or neighbor whose pets keep having litters. Remember, for every pet you buy—a shelter pet will die.

Off topic a bit, but I must bring this up: Some breeders (and I am talking about the *real* breeders) are outraged at the "animal rights'" people who they think want to spay and neuter everything that moves. I know many of these "real breeders" who care deeply about the lineage and the animals themselves. These "real breeders" believe animal rights' people need to shut-up and leave them alone. What many don't understand is that we are all on the same side of the cage.

As an animal advocate myself, I know that "animal rights" people are fighting to stop the indiscriminate breeders who run puppy mills—the backyard breeders and puppy warehouses that supply pet stores with diseased and poorly bred animals—and to stop those who sell their "wares" on street corners and out of cars in parking lots. To all of these so-called breeders, pets are just cash in a cage. It is *these* breeders we are against. Animal rights people are animal lovers, too. Do you think they never want to look into the pond-sized eyes of a *true* bloodhound again? Do you suppose they don't appreciate the tall, elegant stance of a *real* standard poodle? Do you assume they wouldn't miss the silly antics of a *pure* Jack Russell terrier? They are not trying to stop the very rare, true, passionate, careful, honest, caring breeders who have helped these animals maintain their lineage throughout history—they simply want to stop the same people that *the real breeders should want to stop.* They want to stop the heritage-damaging, destructive, careless, greedy, sloppy individuals who have torn the genetics of these fantastic animals down, and have given breeds a bad name. They want to stop those who care nothing about what they can do for the breed, but care only about what that breed can do for them. I believe that removing these destructive, indiscriminate breeders and leaving the handful of the real breeders would do a lot to stop the overflow of pets in this country.

We are all on the same side of the doggie run. We need to work together, all for the same cause. Sermon over. Where was I …?

Okay, speaking of pet shops, here's some great news: The Arizona Humane Society opened a "Petique," a boutique featuring cages full of the dogs and cats from their shelter, located in the upscale Biltmore Shopping Mall in Phoenix. For once, you can go to a pet store and buy shelter pets. It's a smash success and perfect for the many people who want to rescue an animal, but cannot bear to go to the pound. Hopefully this will catch on nationwide.

Check out www.dogsindanger.com. See a photo and the dog's data, including number of days left to live. Another great site is www.petfinders.com, a nationwide *free* service listing thousands of pets waiting for a home. For a look at rescue today, check out: karensrescuelist@yahoogroups.com

To really fight the system, never drop your voiceless animal at the pound to begin with. As the saying goes: How many people does it take to euthanize a pet? Two—someone to give the injection and one uncaring owner.

Don't buy into the myth that pets in pounds are "there for a reason." Don't believe that they're all sock-stealing, shoe-chewing delinquents that'll pee on your curtains. Most are victims of foreclosure, divorce, animal abuse, or uncaring owners. Many are highly cherished companions that simply got lost. No excuses, please—go save a life and find your new heartthrob.

Got a truck? Don't let dogs ride in the back of your pickup. Dr. Deb Zoran, a Texas A&M University veterinary professor, says: "We see numerous cases of injured dogs who have been hurt because they were riding in pickup trucks. And very often, the dog is killed or has to be put to sleep." She recommends crating or tying the dog down with some type of harness or restraint.

Never leave your pet in a car on warm days. Keep your eye out as you walk through parking lots—any dogs (or babies) left inside? In minutes—*minutes*—your car can be hot enough to kill them.

Make sure your pets have collars and microchips with current info. Update, update, update. ID on your pet is also a great help to the generous stranger who took 'em in and is trying to find you. Give them your info so they don't have to put out ads and posters around town. They are trying to help you—make it easy for them.

Never leave your pet unmonitored. To a random source dealer, your pet is fast money on a leash.

Carry a bag of dry dog and cat food in your trunk and leave some when you see strays living on the streets, or in parks, parking lots, anywhere.

Team up with a local store and start a pet food bank for animals. In early 2010 Pet-Co began a national pet food bank, placing giant intake boxes in their stores where people can drop off food to be distributed to local pet groups and to assist pet owners suffering financially.

Or start your own drive. Or help me! Here's an idea I started years ago: Abandon-aid. (With a giant colorful kid's Band-aid with dogs and cats decorating it). You can do this in your local supermarket. Collect food and *everything else* pet groups need, from used (or new) leashes, bowls, bedding, towels, etc. Assign a different local pet organization each month. The chosen group is responsible for picking up all the items daily. No shipping, no storage, and choosing a different group monthly, you share the wealth. Fantastico! Love it. If you want to help (or own a national chain of supermarkets) contact me.

Help local rescuers take care of a feral cat colony.

Suspicious of the workings at your local pound? File for its paperwork under the Freedom of Information Act (FOIA). They must supply you with their records; it's a federal law. (I know people who have done this—it works.)

Talk to local lawmakers to change state laws and regulations. Check laws at www.animallaw.info. To reach your local representatives, go to www.congress.org. To contact all national media, go to www.congress.org/congressorg/dbq/media. (Local and national TV, radio, newspapers and magazines are listed.)

When you see free-to-a-good-home ads on in the newspaper, or on Craigslist, warn the poster. Often those giving away litters do not know about random source dealers and will stop their ads.

Consider becoming a photographer, Internet cross-poster, puller, transportation coordinator, driver, or foster home.

If you live in Arizona, Sheriff Joe Arpaio has a pet posse you can join and help deputies and animal rescuers in Maricopa County. Not in Arizona? See what your local county is doing to stop abuse.

If you're a sheriff or lawmaker, consider a program like Sheriff Joe's MASH (Maricopa Animal Safe Hospice) unit, a no kill shelter for abused pets run and maintained by inmates. His inmates care for abused animals, as the pets' future is decided by the courts. It's win-win for the pets and the inmates. Contact: www.msco. org, MASH Unit. (Only a few other prison systems in the nation allow inmates to care for animals. Immediately following Katrina, the inmates at the Dixon Correctional Institute in Baton Rouge, Louisiana took some of the overflow of pets from the HSUS rescue center in nearby Gonzales, Louisiana.)

FEMA offers *free* online classes and certification so you can help animals in disasters. Check out FEMA independent study at www.training.fema.gov/IS/

Don't feed wild animals; they quickly come to expect to have dinner served, which is detrimental to their long-term survival.

Always put birds back in their nest. Contrary to old wives' tales (a guy surely came up with that) mother birds cannot count or smell, so they don't know their nest was touched and a birdie was tossed in.

Never buy an exotic pet.

Elephants weren't born to wear a baseball cap and swing a bat, and bears don't normally do the cha-cha-cha in the wild. Circuses are not fun for animals.

Don't buy fur or fur-trimmed items. Many people believe if it's just *fur trim*, it's just leftovers from a fur coat and doesn't cause death. Nope. Fur trim is a top dollar business in itself. Many animals will be killed to keep up the demand for fur cuffs and collars.

Here's where you can shop for critter-free couture: Mooshoes. com; Olsenhaus.com, or buy Stella McCartney, whose designs are all fur, leather and feather free.

Think your car contributes to global warming? Your fork may be worse. According to the Intergovernmental Panel on Climate Change (IPCC), the number one cause of global warming is factory farming, making a 40 percent bigger contribution to climate change than all the world's transportation combined. The Department of Agriculture claims that, on average, Americans will eat over 21,000 entire animals in their lifetime. Consider going vegan or vegetarian. Check out: www.vegan.org. For a free vegetarian starter kit: www.vegkit.org. Here are two of the many great books about animals and our planet: *Diet for a New America*, by John Robbins, or *Eating Animals*, by Jonathan Safran Foer.

Keep your eyes and ears alert to the world around you. Next time you're sitting outside a Starbucks drinking a Frappuccino Grande with extra whipped cream (that's me), notice the animals around you. Abused and neglected animals tell their stories in many ways:

Too skinny	Flea or tick infestations
Missing fur, scars	Afraid of owner, cowering
Aggressive towards owner	Limping
Head shaking (ear mites)	Wounds (watch out for dog fighters)

If an animal is being struck, or a dog is tied to the fence all day with no shelter, call 911.

Never dump your rabbit, duck, horse or any animal to fend for itself. Domestic rabbits and ducks cannot survive in local parks or woods among wild-born animals. Foreclosures caused an alarming rise in dumping horses into deserts and fields. They will die a slow, painful death. (I've been on the board of the International Society for the Protection of Mustangs and Burros for 14 years. (Visit www.ispmb.org for more information.) America's wild horses are being rounded up and shipped to Canada and Mexico for slaughter—they desperately need help too.)

Your Skills Are Needed:

Donate prizes, or skills, that can be sold in silent auctions or fund-raisers. Items can be arts and crafts, home décor, collectibles— there are probably lots of goods or services you can donate. (Salons donate haircuts and manicures; plastic surgeons donate skin peels and Botox treatments; print shops, restaurants, hotels, day care—no matter what you do, there's something of value to others.)

Volunteer your services. Carpenters, publicists, copywriters, vet techs, photographers—whatever your talents, there's a rescue nearby that needs your help. If you're a techie like a blogger or Web designer, you can help without leaving home. Writers can help write newsletters and clever pet descriptions to show off a pet's personality.

Everyone is needed on the team. Forever homes, foster homes, drivers, lawyers, dog trainers, dog walkers, cat petters, groomers, vets, computer geeks, and many more—there's a place for everyone.

NOTE: Help for rescuers: To prepare for the next disaster, PetSmart launched an Emergency Relief Waggin'®, providing emergency supplies for pets and rescuers within 48 hours of receiving a request.   www.petsmartcharities.org.

CALLING ALL PILOTS: Pilots N Paws is looking for general aviation pilots to join their 501(c)3 nonprofit program. Make your next flight tax deductible and help rescue animals in need. Go to pilotsnpaws.org to find out how you can help. (Commercial pilots are needed as well.) Another group always in need of airline personnel is Continental's Airline Ambassadors at www.airlineamb.org

CALLING ALL DRIVERS and TRUCKERS: On the road? Transporters are needed across the USA. Take a pet with you and assist in its journey from the pound to its new owner. Here are just a few of the many groups that need your help: www.roadsofhope.org; www.trucknpaws.com; www.operationroger.rescuegroups.org. There are many others that need help, so please Google for them.

GULF OIL SPILL

As this book goes to print, the Gulf needs your help once again. Many unemployed Gulf residents are now abandoning their animals to local shelters. For updates, check out: www. GulfCoastDogsandCats.com; and please donate to Gulf shelters, such as www.animalrescueneworleans.org.

**Thank you for reading this book
and for giving a damn about the animals
we share our planet with.**

If you'd like to contact me, you can reach me at:
ko@orphansofkatrina.com
or
www.orphansofkatrina.com

Books are available at your local bookstore, Amazon.com,
or at buybooks@orphansofkatrina.com

Happy tails to you, from KO …
… and my dog, Little Boy Rudy, and his cats: Splashes,
King Kong, Hi Bobbie, and Sexy Rexy.

Not to forget all the rest—a wink to all the horses, dogs, cats, birds, turtles, mice, fish, lightning bugs, ladybugs, and butterflies that fascinated me throughout my life. And to my longtime companion, my monkey, Martin, that I had to leave behind years ago in the Amazon. And finally, to the sweetest, most trusting feline I have ever known, my darling hippy child, BamBam, recently killed by a pit bull.

About the Author

Karen is a native New Yorker. Born in the Bronx, she spent most of her life traveling around the world picking up languages and speeding tickets. She is a member of the Writers' Guild of America, and was awarded the prestigious Academy of Motion Picture Arts and Sciences' Nicholl Fellowship for screenwriting.

LaVergne, TN USA
23 August 2010
194274LV00005B/6/P